Local Heri

CW01391678

This book by the Coleshill Civic Society's Georgian Group was funded by the Local Heritage Initiative (LHI), a national grant scheme which helps local groups to investigate their landscape and culture. The Local Heritage Initiative is a partnership between the Heritage Lottery Fund, Nationwide Building Society and the Countryside Agency.

Cover Picture:
Coaching from the Swan Inn, Coleshill
By David Rees.

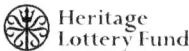

Heritage Lottery Fund

Nationwide

The Countryside Agency

GEORGIAN COLESHILL

By

The Georgian Group of Coleshill Civic Society

Coleshill Market Hall, stocks and pillory in Georgian Times

1

Editor: Sally Jones

Technical Editor: John Hoyle

Art Editor: David Rees

Printer: BIG in INK Ltd

0800 085 1518

Published by Coleshill Civic Society

The Old Market Hall

1, Church Hill

Coleshill

Warwickshire

B46 3AD

First Published 2003

ISBN Number: 0-9545678-0-3

GEORGIAN COLESHILL

Chapter		Page
	INTRODUCTION	4
	by Sally Jones	
1.	POPULATIONS AND OCCUPATIONS	9
	by Peter Rafferty	
2.	ROADS, TURNPIKES AND MAPS	17
	by Elizabeth Waters	
3.	STAGE COACHING AND THE ROYAL MAIL	32
	by Sheila Mitchell	
4.	CANALS AND RAILWAYS	41
	by Jack Stuart	
5.	COLESHILL'S GEORGIAN FAMILIES	46
	by Jack Stuart	
6.	GEORGIAN HOUSES	61
	by Colin Hayfield	
7.	THE INNS OF GEORGIAN COLESHILL	71
	by Jack Stuart	
8.	TRADES AND OCCUPATIONS	81
	by Mavis Cave	
9.	AGRICULTURE	97
	by Elizabeth Waters	
10.	CHURCHES	112
	by Sylvia Hartop	
11.	SCHOOLS	118
	by Andrew Watkins	
12.	LAW, ORDER, CRIME AND PUNISHMENT	124
	by Yvonne Wareing & Margaret Smith	
13.	CHARITIES	141
	by Gabriele Wilson	
14.	THE POOR OF COLESHILL	145
	by Val Preece, Mary Austin & Gwen Bingham	
15.	CONCLUSION TO GEORGIAN COLESHILL	159
	by Elizabeth Waters & Jack Stuart	
	BIBLIOGRAPHY AND SOURCES	163

INTRODUCTION

"The past is a foreign country. They do things differently there."
L.P.Hartley, 'The Go-Between.'

Although nowadays Coleshill is encircled by a tarmac ring of motorways and the tower blocks and maisonettes of Chelmsley Wood, the town retains much of its gracious, old world charm. The parish church crowns the hill, a majestic landmark for miles around. Scores of fine Georgian houses nestle among the traffic bollards and building societies of the High Street while the ancient inns, like 'The Swan' and 'The Coach' evoke the stirring era of stage coaches when the town was a major stop on the mail route from London to Liverpool and Holyhead.

It is a mistake however, to envisage the Georgian era as a rustic golden age or an animated version of the quaint scenes depicted on tins of Quality Street chocolates, all carriages, dashing captains and ladies in muffs and bonnets. Certainly these existed but in the context of tough, uncertain times. The work of Coleshill Civic Society's Georgian Group, delving into sheaves of ancient manuscripts, accounts and records, many of them newly unearthed, is an attempt to strengthen our links with the past and help us to make the imaginative leap towards a realisation of what life was really like for our forbears in the 18th and early 19th centuries.

Among the finds, details of Coleshill's first Wesleyan Chapel and the provision made for the handful of dissenters in the area, thanks to a chance discovery of a bundle of deeds. Painstaking detective work in many of the town's Georgian houses has revealed remnants of even earlier buildings behind the fine facades. The hard life of Sarah Hartill, a pauper, with her escapes from the workhouse, illegitimate children and quests for their putative fathers emerges intriguingly from the parish records. Could this have been a local good-time girl desperate for a livelier existence than the one dictated by her crushing poverty?

This was certainly a society far closer to the edge than our own, the stocks and whipping post in Church Hill and folk memories of the workhouse in Blythe Road providing a reminder of its harshness. There were few of the welfare state safety nets we enjoy and little

4

sympathy for poverty or weakness; petty pilfering would have earned a thrashing or a shameful spell in the stocks, a desperate pauper liberating a rabbit or partridge from milord's acres to feed his starving family could have faced transportation to America.

In this deeply hierarchical era, alternative lifestyles met with equal intolerance. The Georgian equivalent of our New Age travellers were branded rogues and vagabonds; single parents and their offspring would have been stigmatised as unmarried mothers and bastards and a sharp line was drawn between the deserving and the undeserving poor.

The harshness of the ordinary people's existence comes as a shock to most members of today's society where a TV and video recorder are considered necessities. It is salutary to consider the grinding lack of luxury in a household where the labourer father would earn around £50 a year, £36 of which would be spent on bread.

Death and disease were commonplace and the pauper children in particular succumbed with tragic regularity, as the unemotional bulk orders for small coffins show. Medical breakthroughs were already under way, however; the town's celebrated physician-philosopher Dr John Barker advocating inoculation against smallpox even before Edward Jenner's discovery of vaccination. By 1832, we learn that members of Coleshill's delightfully-named Lying In Society, a charity to help women around the time of childbirth, were threatened with expulsion if they did not have their babies vaccinated by the age of 6 months.

This book is intended both as an historical document and a record of some of the human stories and the fascinating local events played out against the rapidly-changing backdrop of Georgian England. It is the result of many hours of research by dedicated volunteers in archives and records offices and in many of the town's shops and fine private houses which represent its glorious Georgian past.

TIME LINE FOR THE GEORGIAN PERIOD 1714-1830

1714 George I comes from Hanover (Germany) to take the English throne. He is unpopular but Protestant.

1715 The Catholic Stuarts (Jacobites) want James III to be king. They rebel but are defeated.

1717 Golden Guinea, price fixed at 21 shillings.

1727 George II comes to the throne but spends much time in Germany.

1728 Court Leet meets in Coleshill

1729 A Turnpike Act passed to repair the road from Stonebridge, Coleshill to the city of Chester.

1739 Dick Turpin hanged at York.

1745 Bonnie Prince Charlie, the last of the Stuart family, tries to claim the British throne with another Jacobite rebellion. They are beaten.

1750 First organised Police Force in London - the Bow Street Runners.

1760 George III (known as Farmer George) comes to the throne. He is popular, but suffers from ill health.

1760 New Turnpike road built from Stonebridge to Coleshill.

1760 Market Cross built in Church Hill with pillory and stocks.

1765 St. Leonard's Church, Over Whitacre is built.

1769 A new master appointed for Coleshill Grammar School to teach 20 poor boys for £5 a year.

1770 Captain Cook claims Australia for Britain.

1775 American colonies rebel against Britain.

1779 The Enclosure Commissioners meet at the Swan Inn.

1783 Estate map of Coleshill by John Snape.

1784 The first mail coach leaves Bristol at 4.00pm and arrives in London the next morning before 8.00am.

1789 The Hon. John Byng describes the Swan Inn as shabby and dull.

1789 Beginning of the French Revolution.

1793 Start of the Napoleonic Wars.

1797 Time bills for the Royal Mail coach from London to Liverpool show a delivery at the Swan Inn at 10.45am.

1798	Birmingham and Fazeley Canal opens, passing through Curdworth.
1798	Coleshill Grammar School has a new brewhouse and a coal house.
1798	Steam powered spinning mill opens in Bradford.
1800	Population of Coleshill is 1035.
1801	Ireland joins Great Britain.
1804	First steam locomotive invented by Richard Trevithick.
1805	British Navy wins the battle of Trafalgar against the French, Lord Nelson dies.
1806	Steam powered looms invented.
1807	Slave trading abolished.
1810	John Mason, Coleshill's first Methodist granted the right to use a house for public worship by the Bishop of Lichfield.
1811	National Census records population of Coleshill as 1639.
1811	The 'Luddites', out of work weavers, wreck looms.
1815	Britain defeats Napoleon at the battle of Waterloo.
1816	National Game Law Act limits the right to game to landowners only.
1819	Peterloo Massacre, near Manchester.
1819	Illegal for children under nine to be put to work.
1820	George III dies, George IV now king
1821	National Census records Population of Coleshill as 1760.
1822	George Salmon appointed Headmaster of Coleshill Grammar School. Annual salary of £80 to teach and instruct all the boys of the parish.
1825	First steam passenger railway driven from Stockton to Darlington.
1826	Wesleyan Chapel and its members fully established.
1830	George IV dies and the Georgian Era ends. Coleshill's coaching trade in decline.
1830	King William IV takes the throne.
1836	The workhouse at Coleshill closes.
1837	Queen Victoria comes to the throne.

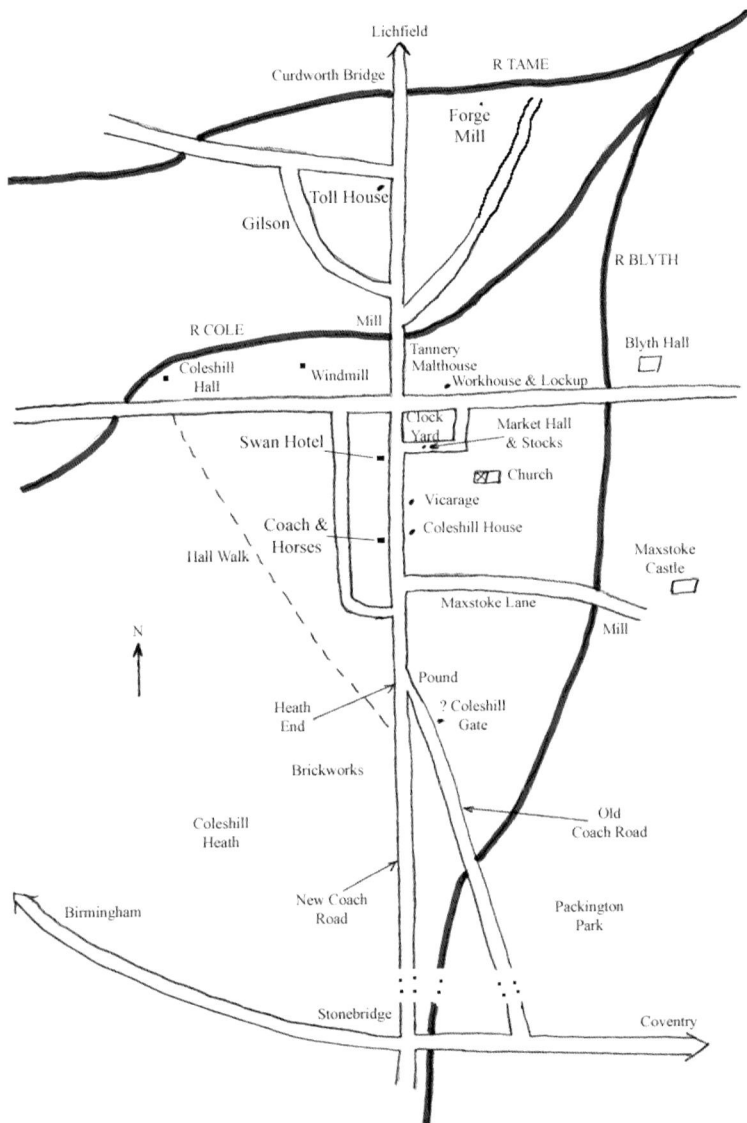

A plan of Georgian Coleshill. (not to scale)

Chapter 1

POPULATION AND OCCUPATIONS

Coleshill remained a picturesque and prosperous market town mainly dependent on agriculture throughout the Georgian period. It was notable for its splendid church and the range of fine houses occupied by the Lords of the Manor and the local gentry, but it experienced the same political and social changes that caused such upheaval throughout the rest of Britain. There was a sense of new beginnings; the growth of Empire, the expansion of foreign trade, the start of the Industrial Revolution and a new Royal House.

While the population rose throughout the country; from 9 million in 1750, to 11 million in 1801 and up to 16.5 million by 1831, the biggest increase was in rural areas and Coleshill reflected the trend, its population almost doubling from 975 to 1853. Agriculture and domestic service were the town's main occupations and the lowest paid. The 1831 census records that 30% of the adult population was employed in these, almost a third of the men over 20 working as agricultural labourers. Only 23 families occupied land

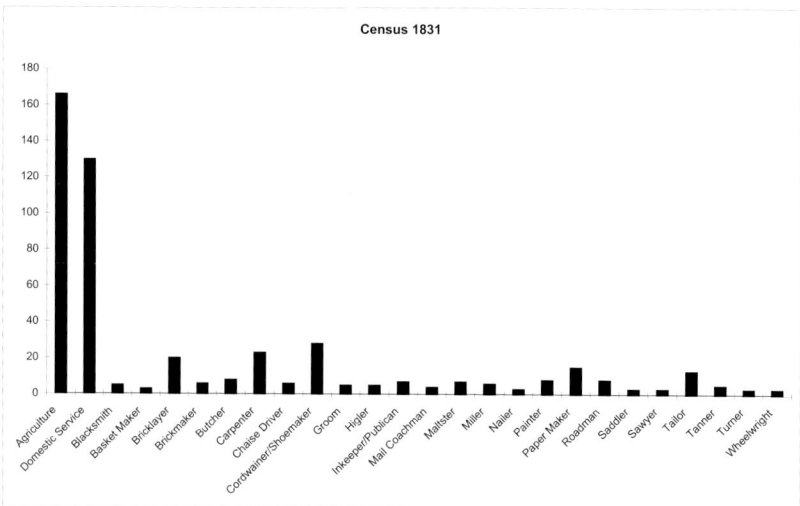

Census 1831

and just 6 of these worked it without outside help.

There were 126 other occupations with the number of tradespeople up to 221 by 1830. This group, which generally enjoyed a good income and high social status, was mainly composed of trades supporting agriculture but included retailers. The number and variety of *"Shopkeepers, Traders &c"* listed in 'Pigot's Directory of Warwickshire' suggests a lively retail trade. Among the higher income groups were *"Clergy, Clerks, Professional and other educated men"* and *"Gentlemen and Gentlewomen"*, totalling 24 by 1831.

FARMING

Many changes took place in farming with the further development of enclosure and the introduction of mechanical methods. By the end of the period, the remaining medieval fields and commons were enclosed but while this radically improved farming methods, it eliminated common grazing rights, a major hardship to farm labourers. The cost of fencing tiny plots made smaller units uneconomic for small farmers, causing widespread unemployment and poverty among those who would previously have raised a handful of pigs and cattle or planted subsistence crops on their own few acres.

By the end of the period most farm workers were day labourers, enjoying far better conditions than live-in workers who were usually hired for 6 months and agreed a lump sum at the start, in addition to their keep. They were not paid until the end of the period, restrictive terms which ensured that most were young and single.

Day labourers rented their cottages and were paid a much higher proportion of their wages in cash, making marriage possible. Their income was unreliable as they could often be laid off when bad weather halted outside work and most families experienced spells of hunger when they had to depend on charity or Poor Relief.

Through increased specialisation during the late 18th and early 19th centuries, labour requirements peaked at certain times of the year which made farmers less inclined to hire farm-help and encouraged the transition from farm-service to day labouring. This shift continued as the more prosperous farmers opted for greater privacy by not having their employees in their homes.

Farmers' fortunes varied considerably and they were not uniformly wealthy, the majority having a comfortable rather than lavish lifestyle. A contemporary farming journalist defined three categories of Norfolk farmers:

- The lowest class lived and dined with their servants and farm workers.

- The second class lived in the kitchen with their servants but dined at a separate table.

- The highest class no longer lived in the kitchen and had separate spacious apartments.

EARNINGS AND LIVING STANDARDS

Wage differentials in the Georgian period were similar to those of today and there were three main rules of thumb:

- Craftsmen's wages were higher than labourers'.

- Wages in London for both categories were higher than in the Provinces.

- Men were more highly paid than women, even for similar or identical work

The levels of real wages rose only slowly during the early part of the period because good harvests produced low cereal prices during the first half of the 18th century. Many workers' earnings peaked in 1792, after which population growth, poorer harvests, a changing labour market due to the increased labour force and the French wars brought major changes which kept wages low. The only exceptions to this were in parts of the Midlands and North where manufacturing change and expansion created different local labour markets.

This table gives an idea of typical wages for the period from 1730 to 1780:

Job	Wage	Today's equivalent
Bricklayer	3s per week	£18
Bricklayer's Mate	2/6d per week	£15
Cotton Weaver	7s per week	£42
Framework Knitter	6s per week	£36
Foreman Forester	1/6d per day	£9
Hand Loom Weaver	7/6d per week	£45
Labourer	3d per day	£1.80
Saddler	12s per week	£72
Tailor	9s per week	£54

Many workers augmented their earnings by taking additional jobs and often several members of a family worked and contributed to the household income.

Lord Digby's Sherborne Estate paid the following yearly wages in 1763:

Job	Wage	Today's equivalent
Bailiff	£30	£3750
Cook	£18	£2175
Gardener	£20	£2420
Keeper	£11	£2330
Under Groom	£3. 5s	£395
Postillion	£3	£365
Shepherd	£16	£1940
Maid	£4	£484

These wages were earned on a large estate; a cook-general in service to a middle class family could earn as little as £4.10s (Current value £545) per year. During the following analysis, the current values are included in brackets after the contemporary figure and denote the equivalent purchasing power of the £ in 2001.

The earnings of farmers varied substantially. In 1759 the majority (77%) of tenant farmers earned £40 (£4840) per year with the top 3% earning £150 (£18,150). The majority of freeholders earned £25 (£3,025) per year, less than many urban artisans and indeed less than some cottage ale sellers. 43% earned between £50 (£6,050) and £100 (£12,100) By 1801 the average for all tenant farmers was £120 (£5,050) with 25% of freeholders earning £200 (£8,400) and the majority earning £90 (£3,800).

PROFESSIONS

Historically the term profession meant the same as occupation or simply employment. During the 18th century the term began to acquire a more precise meaning and to refer to occupations requiring training in specialist knowledge used to provide a service. There were no set scales of pay and earnings varied considerably.

TEACHERS

There were no formal entry qualifications and it was not a lucrative, full-time occupation, many masters having second jobs. A master running a private urban school could earn £40 (£4,840) per year but a village schoolmaster could be paid as little as £6 (£725). In 1763 this was the salary which Lord Digby paid to the master at Sheldon School. In 1784 Mary Wilcox was paid £3 (£365) per year for instructing poor children at Marston Green.

LAWYERS

Again there was no scale of fees or typical payment but an established lawyer could achieve a good income. Having completed his training, a lawyer who could not set up his own practice would continue as a journeyman clerk when (in 1747) he could earn a wage of 10/6 (£63) per week.

SURGEONS

The most common route into this profession was not via university but through an apprenticeship to a surgeon. As with lawyers, most entrants came from the lesser gentry and the middle classes. A hard-working doctor could make a reasonable living but had to operate on a commercial basis. This could create customer resistance and in 1760 a shopkeeper noted resentfully in his diary that his doctor had charged 10/6d (£63) for a visit.

LIVING STANDARDS

Price rises affected living standards far more than wage movements, as 80% of working-class incomes was spent on food, mostly bread, so the well-being of the poor depended on the corn harvest. Higher food prices caused by the lack of corn following poor harvests increased the pressure on already low incomes, with disastrous results. Poverty and hunger triggered protests and there were food riots in many regions, including the Midlands, during fourteen periods between 1727 and 1818. The war which started in 1793 sent corn prices soaring by 50% in the space of a year. The subsequent famine caused rioting in Birmingham and Coventry and Coleshill was almost certainly affected.

To gauge living standards effectively it is necessary to relate earnings to household expenditure. Two examples of rural labourers' budgets are:

BERKSHIRE: Household of husband, wife and four children

TOTAL INCOME from all sources per year	£46 (£5565)
EXPENDITURE	
Bread	£36
Other foodstuffs and expenses	£16
TOTAL EXPENDITURE	£52 (£6290)
DEFICIT:	£6 (£725)

The family would not eat fresh meat or potatoes.

NORTHAMPTONSHIRE: Household of husband, wife and five children

TOTAL INCOME from all sources per year	£27 (£3265)
TOTAL EXPENDITURE (excluding heating)	£28 (£3385)
DEFICIT	£1 (£120)

In addition fuel costs could amount to £2.10s (£305) per year.

The estimated expenditure necessary to maintain a middle class family of husband, wife, four children and a maidservant is £390 (£47,200) per year, including 4s (£24) per week pocket money for the master.

SOCIAL HIERARCHY

The social hierarchy in rural areas during the Georgian Period was rigidly determined, changing little in districts untouched by industrialisation. The factors governing the make-up of the hierarchical pyramid were social position and wealth, which kept the largest social group, labourers and domestic servants, at the bottom.

LANDOWNERS
CLERGY   GENTRY
FARMERS PROFESSIONS
TRADESMEN:
SHOPKEEPERS WHEELWRIGHTS BLACKSMITHS CARPENTERS
LABOURERS DOMESTIC SERVANTS
PAUPERS

The labourers and domestic servants, although the largest single social group, had little or no contact with the others. The living standards of the gentry, landowners and middle classes are well recorded in historical accounts and fiction. Novelists like Jane Austen and George Eliot have given detailed information of their way of life and strict social hierarchy, but little first-hand information survives of the daily lives of labourers and their families. This social group had limited opportunity for education. As no public money was spent on elementary education in England, it was mainly provided by charity schools, dame schools and latterly by the Sunday School Movement. Children did not qualify for schooling until the age of 6 and as they were likely to be working by the age of 9 and 10, generally had only a rudimentary education. Lack of compulsion meant that some would receive no education. Standards of teaching were variable and often poor. Some groups also believed that it was unnecessary or even dangerous to educate the poor except for teaching them the skills and knowledge they needed in their working lives.

JOSEPH ARCH, founder of the Agricultural Workers Union, was born at Barford, Warwickshire in 1826 and in his autobiography he vividly describes how, during his childhood, everyone was required to keep to their station; even when taking Communion :

"First up walked the Squire to the communion rails; the farmers went up next; then up went the tradesmen, the shopkeepers, the wheelwright and the blacksmith; and then, the very last of all, went the poor agricultural labourers in their smock frocks. They walked up by themselves; nobody else knelt with them; it was as if they were unclean."

Housing followed the same pattern: rich and increasingly successful people built new houses or renovated their existing ones. Many fine Georgian buildings remain in Coleshill as well as other buildings which were extended and re-fronted during the period. The town was described as *"a considerable thoroughfare"* in 1822 and the combination of gentry, farmers, tradesmen and professionals suggests that this was a thriving community. The standard of labourers' cottages varied widely, from the well-built to those described by WILLIAM COBBET in Rural Rides (1830):

"Hovels, made of mud and of straw, bits of glass or of old cast of windows, without frames or hinges, frequently, but merely stuck in the mud walls ..bits of chairs or stools; wretched boards tacked together to serve for a table; the floor of pebble broken brick, or of bare ground;...a thing called a bed and rags on the backs of the wretched inhabitants."

As almost no labourers' cottages of the period remain, we can only hope that Coleshill boasted few of the type which Cobbett described, although the number of paupers recorded must mean that many people lived in pitiful conditions.

CHAPTER 2

ROADS, TURNPIKES AND MAPS

Travelling along the main route through Coleshill today, you notice recognisable Georgian features in many of the houses, hotels and inns. Some seem quite grand for what would then have been a small but flourishing market town. From registered baptisms, which are often unreliable, the population fluctuated between 810 and 1035 from the year 1712 until 1800. The census records give the total number of persons in 1811 as 1639, rising a decade later to 1760 and a decade after that to 1892. These figures are considered to be more accurate as they were gathered for the government.

The last 30 years of the Georgian period showed a significant increase in the population, almost a third of whom worked primarily in agriculture. The fine houses and other buildings indicate rising prosperity and the population definitely increased. But why? Among the possible answers are Coleshill's strategic position on the Great North Road to Liverpool, North Wales and Ireland, and improved communications such as the turnpiking of several existing roads plus the new road built between the south end of Coleshill and Meriden in 1760. The crucial question is whether the accident of geography and improved communications were directly responsible for the population increase and Coleshill's status as a prosperous Georgian market town.

Britain's communication systems developed through the ages into an interlocking system of trade routes, large and small, which ran between centres of production and consumption, between village and village, between town and countryside, between port and hinterland. In the 18th century, the land was sparsely and patchily populated by around seven million people, three quarters of them still working and living on the land. Inland transport was still mainly dictated by geography; the lie of the land and the physical barriers which controlled how far people travelled, where to and at what time of year.

Trade in and out of towns and markets had remained almost unchanged since medieval times. It was no surprise to find wheeled vehicles alongside the geese, cattle and sheep still being herded

17

along the old drove roads. These were the wide, grassy tracks by which animals were driven from hill pastures to new fattening pastures and later to the great markets of the Midlands and eventually London. Coleshill was on the main 13th century drove road from Wales to the Midlands, and, like many similar tracks, it became increasingly important, particularly for drovers in the 18th century because it was not subject to tolls.

Navigable waterways complemented road travel, but Coleshill had neither navigable rivers nor canals so transport to and from the town was all by road. The condition of the roads was a matter of luck and geography. In medieval times, improvements mainly involved replacing wooden bridges with stone ones which were usually narrow, with recesses to shelter pedestrians from the traffic. The bridges were only replaced if the roads either side were significant, Coleshill bridge at the foot of the town being a typical example.

Local people maintained their own roads, and the upkeep of the highways was the responsibility of the manorial courts. The Highways Act of 1555 appointed surveyors of highways, the first legislation ever passed applying to English roads in general, and assigned responsibility for roads to the community, a ruling which remained until 1835.

With a network still based on the Roman system linking London with the provinces, some communities were hard pressed to maintain their roads, as there was much greater mobility in some areas than others. Unwilling parishioners were responsible for road maintenance. The growing traffic on the roads however created increasing problems, such as holloways; sunken tracks produced by continuous wear on a dip, ditch or road, throwing the earth up into high banks on either side, often narrowing the tracks. This erosion of unmade surfaces or wide morasses created difficult conditions especially on sloping ground. Vehicles were mainly packhorses and carts and the town streets were pot-holed, narrow and strewn with debris.

Markets added to the erosion of roads and market stalls generated rubbish. Parishes and the government tried to subsidise the roads by imposing tolls or restricting loads. The Highways Act of 1662 prohibited wagons drawn by more than seven-horse teams or fitted with wheels less than four inches wide. Tolls were not new, but they had traditionally been for bridges. In 1663 the first turnpike Act tolled part of the Great North Road, one of the major routes used by the 17th and 18th century diarists who gave us a vivid insight into travel conditions.

JOHN LELAND, who was employed by Henry VIII to compile an 'Itinerary of Britain', visited the area early in the 16th century and described Coleshill as:

"A praty thrwgh-farre in Werwikeshire, leyinge by northe and southe up an hill, hathe but one longe sttrete and a paroche churche, at the southe end of it. It is countyd almoste the middle betwixt Tamworthe and Coventry".

Travelling was often uncomfortable and dangerous. RALPH THORSBY noted in his diary of 1680 that a traveller could find himself lost on the Great North Road itself or riding with his saddlebags in floodwater. Roads had actually deteriorated since the Middle Ages and the increase in wheeled traffic was rapidly making them worse still. Most goods were transported by long strings of pack animals and travel was mainly on horseback.

Around 1635 the stagecoach began to supersede the wains or long wagons, which had served as long-distance transport for rich and poor passengers alike since the middle of the 14th century. Private carriages were becoming increasingly important, as was stagecoaching, though only for a small handful of travellers. However it was not until the late 18th and early 19th centuries that the real boom in coaching began. By then the road improvements had reduced travel times but not necessarily its discomfort. The road conditions depended wholly on the type of soil in the area and right up to the time of Telford and McAdam, roads in clay country were often impassable after heavy rain. London could be virtually cut off from the North by the belt of clay in the Midlands.

CELIA FIENNES was born on June 7th 1662 at Newton Toney near Salisbury. She lived at a time when many antiquaries and topographers were writing about the English past and people kept and published journals of their travels. Unlike Daniel Defoe, a government agent, she saw at first hand everything she described; she was in no one's employ and was a wholly detached and independent witness. Almost all her journeys were made on horseback and on her 'Great journey' of 1698, she travelled alone apart from servants, of whom only two are mentioned. She took spare horses with her but never records how many.

When Celia Fiennes undertook the 'Northern Journey and the Tour of Kent' she mentions Coleshill which she approached from Lichfield and records;

"We then went to Colehill (Coleshill) and pass'd several good houses; here I saw the way of makeing Runnett (Rennet) as they do in Cheshire; they take the Reed bag and Curd and having washed it clean, salt it and breake the Curd small about the bag, so drye them being stretched out with sticks like a glove, and so hang them in a chimney till you need it, then cut a piece off this as a big as halfe a crown and boyle it in a little water, which water will turn the milke better than any made runnet and its freshe; this is a pretty little market town and stands on a hill. Thence to Coventry all on a level"

"From Warwick we went towards Daventry all along the Vale of the Red Horse which was a very heavy way and could not reach thither being 14 mile; about 11 mile we came to a place called Nether Shugar (Lower or Nether Shackburgh) a sad village, we could have no entertainment; just by it on the top of a steep hill is Shuggbery Hall a seate of Sir Charles Suggberys, who seeing our distress, being just night and horses weary with the heavy way, he very curteously took compassion on us and treated us very handsomely that night."

Celia Fiennes was fascinated by hearsay and her descriptions of the quirky practices she encountered bring her diaries vividly alive. In 1697 she recorded

*"*The following antient custom I omitted to insert. -'They have an antient custom at Coleshill in the County of Warwick, that if the young men of the town can catch a hare, and bring it to the parson of the parish, before ten of the clock on Easter Monday, the parson is bound to give them a calves head, and a hundred eggs, for their breakfast; and a groat in money'..".*

Sir William Dugdale makes several references in his diaries to travelling from Coleshill to London on the Lichfield and Shrewsbury coaches in the late 1670s.

Few people travelled any distance for pleasure at the turn of the 18th century. Road surfaces varied considerably and the heavy clays rapidly became quagmires in the wet winter season. Many roads were not enclosed with hedges or fences and some were barely-discernable tracks. Maps were almost non-existent and so travel was very uncertain.

The earliest maps showed towns in relation to rivers. Johan Blaeu showed 'Worcester, Warwik Shire, and The Liberty of Coventre' within a river map of the area. One of the earliest road books was John Norden's, 'An Intended Guide for English Travellers', which appeared in 1625. When John Ogilby published his road book 'Brittania' in 1675, it was essentially a map that had been drawn by an anonymous cartographer 300 years earlier. John Ogilby's maps, though published separately from their descriptive matter in 1675, were too large to be easily consulted on the road; early maps were far too bulky for travellers to carry. Henry Beighton's 'Mapp of Warwickshire' surveyed in 1725 was still dominated by 'Rivers Brooks & Rills' but it does include the Roman roads and stations. Many maps were copies and so mistakes and inaccuracies were usually repeated. Milestones first appeared at the end of the seventeenth century and stones were erected along the Great North Road in 1708, thanks to private enterprise. Official milestones were authorised on the London to Chester road in 1744, but did not become compulsory until 1773.

Guide-posts, crosses and pillars pre-dated milestones, some standing several feet high so that horse riders could see them. Until the 20th century, however route details were usually given by word of mouth.

DANIEL DEFOE toured Great Britain as a government agent early in the 18th century and recounted his experiences in 'A Tour through the whole island of Great Britain', published between 1724 and 1726. Defoe described Coleshill as a *"very handsome town on the great road"* and recorded his journey from Dunstable to Chester, through Coventry and Coleshill thus:

"The deep clays reach through all towns of Bickenhill, Fenny and Stony Stratford, Towcester, Daventry, Dunchurch, Coventry, Coleshill and even Birmingham, for very near eighty miles. The deep clays are surprisingly soft that it is a wonder to foreigners, how considering the great number of carriages are continually passing with heavy loads, those ways have been made practicable; indeed the

21

Old Toll House, Jack O'Watton. Corner of Watton Lane and Lichfield Road,

From Grimstock along the turnpike road.

great number of horses every year kill'd by the excess of labour in those ways, has been such a charge to the country."

Defoe's 'great road' linked Holyhead to London and his description shows how busy it was, as well as suggesting that Coleshill was as important as the other towns he listed. He also describes how the turnpiking of such roads provided the money to maintain them and bring them up to the standard of the great Roman roads of the past.

Turnpike Trusts began in the late 17th century and were financed by borrowing and tollgate takings as well as stagecoach duty, which was levied by the Stamp Office, according to the vehicle's seating capacity. Tollgates were built at road junctions and part of the tolls was used to maintain the highway, although parishioner labour was still used. One turnpike, Curdworth Gate, stood at the north end of Coleshill and appeared both in John Snape's 1783 map of the parish, and in later maps drawn by Noble in 1789 and Carey in 1806. The early turnpikes produced very little improvement as they did not bring in much money and there was no re-routing. The details of the legislation make it clear that most of the money collected from the tolls was intended for road repairs:

"During the reign of George II Regis, a Turnpike Act was passed which was to commence and take place from the fifth day of May, which was in the year of our Lord 1729, and from thence to continue in and during the term of twenty-one years."

"An act for more effectually repairing the roads from COLESHILL in the county of WARWICK, through the city of LITCHFIELD, to STONE in the county of Stafford, and from thence to the city of CHESTER, and for amending other roads therein mentioned."

The turnpike road serving Coleshill ran from the town to Cannals post, Lichfield and the trustees' duty was to erect turnpikes and toll houses and collect the appropriate tolls and duties. If anyone tried to evade the toll by unloading goods before the gate or leaving goods in a house, or putting the coach or cattle into another place, then the trustees could fine them ten shillings or impose a forfeit, as the Act made clear.

"The roads would be measured and divided into distances and stones or posts would be erected by the roads with appropriate

marks, words, letters and figures. If anyone voluntarily or maliciously break any of the stones or deface them a penalty would be paid: - replace them, repair them, a sum of twenty shillings, or go to the house of correction at Warwick for a period of six weeks for hard labour."

Coleshill's importance as a coaching route was threatened as early as 1734 when a petition was presented to parliament to turnpike part of Watling Street from Weedon to Nuneaton. Although the petition failed, an Act was passed in 1760-61 to turnpike the road from Coleshill to Chester. Turnpiking usually involved upgrading and slightly altering the existing route. This time, however, an entirely new road was built from the southern end of Coleshill to Meriden Heath, avoiding Packington Park and the River Blythe's flood plain, and joining up with another new route, the Chester Road, from Castle Bromwich to Meriden. John Tomlinson surveyed the intended roads in 1760.

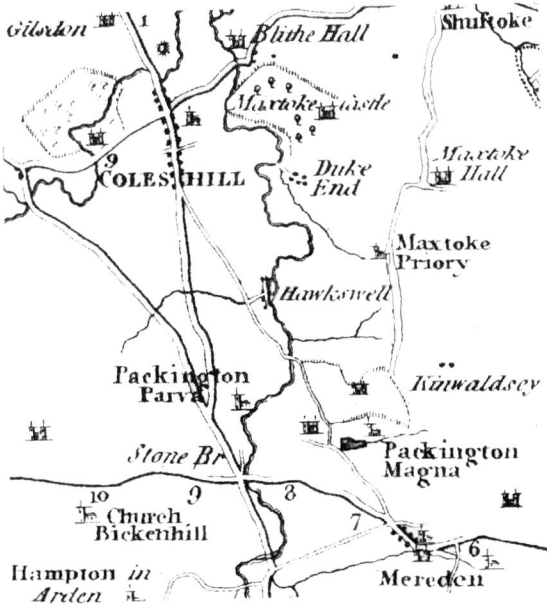

New route and road from Coleshill to Meriden. Noble/Cary 1806

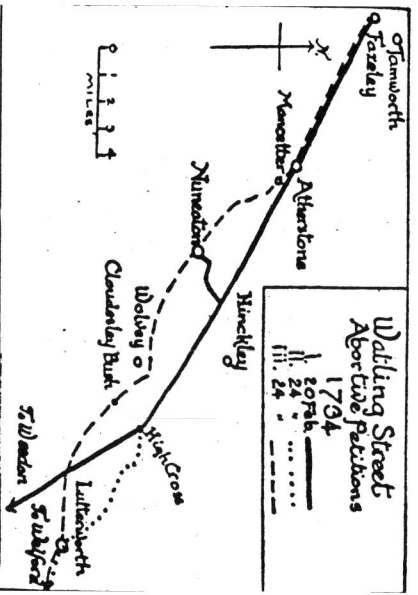

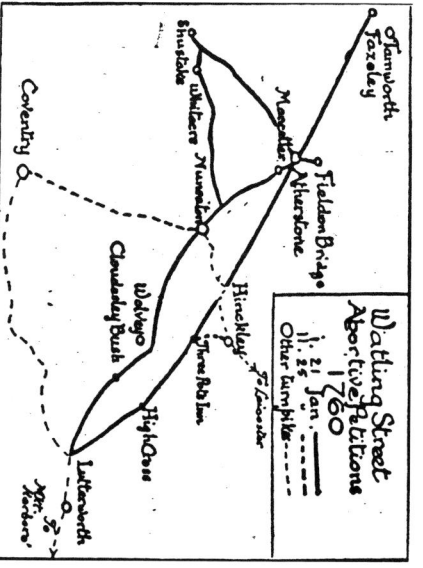

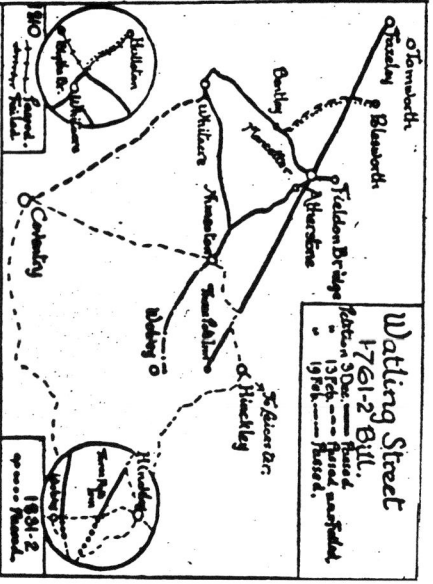

TAKEN FROM "WARWICKSHIRE TURNPIKES"

by Arthur Cossons. Page 63

Extract from Vol. 64 of "Birmingham Archaeological Society's Transactions".

The maps are based on the Ordnance Survey map, with the sanction of H. M. Stationery Office.

The same year another petition was made to turnpike Watling Street amid protests from various quarters including Coleshill. The objectors claimed that the new road would be detrimental ('destructive' appeared in one petition) to the existing main roads and the trade of the towns along them. Watling Street would have acted as a by-pass for the heaviest and most important traffic and the opposition again succeeded in getting the petition dropped. Two years later, however, the Bill was enacted and the Watling Street Trust was formed

This had little immediate impact on Coleshill, but the improvements to Watling Street encouraged other turnpike trusts to follow suit, particularly in areas of heavy clay. In 1829 the 18th edition of 'Paterson's Roads, 1771' by Edward Mogg recorded the transformation of the London to Holyhead road, describing

"the following road in its highly improved state, and exhibiting the projected alterations, which through the Munificence of Parliament, are still in contemplation, under the very able direction of Mr. Telford". There is no doubt that the route through Coleshill was important, but not at a time when people were travelling widely or when it was inexpensive. Roads were turnpiked if they were considered to be economically viable. Despite the Act for the trust in 1729 and the new road skirting Packington in 1760, Coleshill's importance declined steadily as it was bypassed by the main routes which now linked the major expanding cities. Thomas Kitchen's map and route in the 'Travellers Guide to all England and Wales', 1783 gives no real mention of the town, only the route.

THE HON. JOHN BYNG, (later the fifth Viscount Torrington) travelled as a government agent to collect information on the towns, roads and villages of England. His diaries mention Coleshill several times, often unflatteringly.

"Saturday, June 27th, 1789.

A road of retirement, goodness and beauty trail'd us along, passing thro' some small villages, near the church of Whitacre; then cross'd the river where we descry'd before us, the high steeple of Coleshill, and enter'd the Swan Inn at 9 o' clock. This town lying on the Chester road is placed upon a pleasant hill. After a crawl up and down the street, we returned to our dull and shabby inn; so were likewise ourselves, and our supper.'' This comment does not suggest a flourishing coaching town, as there appears to be no choice of inn: *"Sunday, June 28th, 1789.*

When we return'd to our inn, the rain continuing, we debated if it wou'd not be better to make an early dinner, and trust to a fine evening: this determined, we wrote letters, and read newspapers, till the arrival of the very good dinner. This finish'd and the weather clearing up, we continued our ride, back to Blythe Hall, now modernised, wherein formerly Sr Wm Dugdale resided; and then turn'd through fields to Maxstoke Castle, to which we bore an introductory letter from Merevale Hall.''
Wednesday, July 17th 1793.

The heat of the day had too long detain'd me at N-Eaton, for now the days close before expectation; and besides I go very slow. - And country of much greenness, and of timber, led me to a village of [-]; and by nine o'clock, (too late, as you may not secure good beds, and stabling) I arrived at the Swan Inn at Coleshill: Strange - that upon such a road there should be nothing better than an alehouse! To a cold supper, as soon as my horses were bedded in a bad stable:- Poor Flora is quite stiff, and tired. - An old lady was commandant here - as at Harboro', but of cooler breed; - and I dared to order some food for my dog! I am nearly roasted thro; and shall not have one drop of gravy left in me.''

John Byng was evidently no fan of Coleshill's accommodation: *"Thursday, July 18th*

Up at seven o'clock; walk'd around Coleshill Churchyard - an high, and fine spot, whilst my coffee was preparing; and when that was finish'd, (the old horse beans) hasten'd to depart. Passing by the side of Ld. D [igby]'s Park, (which might be restored into a fine place, for a river runs thro' it) and by the old casemented house. - These roads are intolerable - being only mended by round pebbles, that for ever rowl about and I am too nervous for such work.''

Discomfort was not the only hardship which travellers faced: highway robbery was a continuous threat and often organised by gangs. Occasionally coach accidents were caused maliciously. The COVENTRY MERCURY of 9th September 1782 reported:

"Early yesterday morning the Liverpool post coach going between Coleshill and Lichfield was overthrown by some evil minded

27

persons or person laying some timber across the road by which accident the coachman (Samuel Ford) was killed on the spot and a young woman an outside passenger had a leg and arm broke: happily the company within, three persons received no material injury."

The diarists reveal many details of local travel and transport development in the 18th century. The turnpike system reached Warwickshire as early as 1707 and by 1783 Thomas Kitchen recorded in his 'Traveller's Guide through England and Wales' that Coleshill was one of the *"Cities, Towns and Considerable Villages on the High Roads from London."* In the late 18th century its inhabitants could, money permitting, travel all over England, but as travel was expensive, few ventured far from home.

Several of Coleshill's early coaching inns remain, some still displaying the wide arched entrances that once ushered in coaches, horses and passengers. Two of the earliest are the Swan Inn and the former Angel Inn, now a private house, both established early in the 18th century when coaching was just starting.

The fine Swan Coaching Inn

28

74-76 High Street taken in the 1960's, formerly The Angel Inn. The raised part of the white string course represents the High Street side of the coach entrance

The Coach and Horses was built at the end of the century when the industry was booming but few other large establishments or houses were erected in Coleshill at this time.

As Coleshill was a market town it had plenty of horse-related trades, but there is little evidence to show that it was a prosperous coaching town after 1800. At the height of the coaching era, 1800-1830, the population of Coleshill almost doubled, but coaching declined as Coleshill was no longer on a major route. The routes and times given in Pigot and Co.'s Directory for Warwickshire 1828 show that the mail left the Swan Inn daily for Liverpool and London until 1834. However, although Coleshill was an important market town with heavy traffic to and from the local markets of Atherstone, Nuneaton, Birmingham, Coventry and Tamworth, no great industrial expansion took place and this restricted the number of coach services passing through.

Coleshill's improved roads and population increase came about within a 50 year period in which a few new houses were built in the High Street while others received a Georgian 'facelift', their medieval interiors encased in the fashion of the day. Lord Digby, the Lord owned many of these houses. He no longer lived in Coleshill, but during this time, before enclosure became statutory, he had been enclosing his lands and consolidating his farming assets. Some of his tenants continued to rent the larger farms whilst others were forced to move.

Coach Hotel

Many of the bigger farm houses were improved or enlarged. Lord Digby's brother lived in Coleshill House for almost 20 years, as Vicar of Coleshill and Sheldon from 1765 until his death in 1788. His presence boosted the town's status and he espoused the fashions of the day, particularly in architecture and design, a taste probably emulated by the residents. At this era the Coleshill Book Club met at the Swan Inn every month where they dined and borrowed books. There were several well-known members including Mr. Adderley, Mr. Croxall, Mr. D. Digby, and Mr. Ludford of Ansley Hall, the latter two travelling over in their post-chaises.

The first meeting of the Commissioners for the Land Enclosure met at the Swan Inn on March 20th 1779 and John Snape from Wishaw, their surveyor, published his map of the parish in 1783. Mr. John Barker, who lived in the Market Place, was an eminent surgeon, apothecary and author and had many works published between 1769 and 1796. This, plus the growing number of trades, all added to the prosperity of the town, which at the time was on the main coaching route to the Northwest of England, Wales and Ireland.

Although diarists and cartographers included Coleshill on the Great North Road, fostering the belief that its growing prosperity was due to coaching, the population was already increasing steadily in the late 18th century and the majority of the Georgian buildings was well established. The glory of Coleshill as a coaching town was short-lived and according to the available evidence, the population increase after 1800 appears to be almost unconnected with the trade.

Base of Post Windmill c. 1960, Birmingham Road by David Rees.

Stage Coach at full tilt by David Rees.

The Barker Window, Coleshill Church. Photograph by Peter Rafferty.

'The Reverend William Digby,
The Dean of Durham'
by Joshua Reynolds.

Highwaymen were a hazard
to stagecoach travellers
by David Rees

18th century English Mail coach guard, printed 1832.

CHAPTER 3

STAGE COACHING AND THE ROYAL MAIL 1714 – 1831

Between 1770 and 1835 coaching was a major industry and Coleshill, which until around 1800 stood on an important route, benefited from the boom. Stagecoach travel was so called because the journey was made in stages of between 10 and 15 miles. At each stop, the horses were changed and travellers could refresh themselves or stay overnight at an inn and take another coach next day. This often meant sharing a bed with a complete stranger and sometimes smaller and more irritating species. Coleshill's accommodation had a distinctly dodgy reputation. John Byng who stayed at the Swan in 1789 described it as *"dull and shabby."*

The artist J.M.W. Turner often used the coach, always sitting outside at the back regardless of the weather. He travelled north each year on the 'True Briton', 'Highflyer' or 'Lord Nelson'. In one typical journey, he went from London to Grantham on the 12th July, paying 2 shillings and 8 pence in porterage, 5s 6d for dinner and 2 guineas for his fare. He must have enjoyed the journey as he gave a 1s 6d tip and certainly used the Coleshill route because he painted a picture of Coventry.

Coaches were used primarily by the business community, particularly merchants and manufacturers. The service developed in the last quarter of the 18th century in response to the expanding economy, allowing traders to buy and sell when profit margins were greatest and shift goods, orders and bills of payment rapidly around the country. The coaches carried a huge variety of vital commodities; from raw cotton and wool yarn, thread and cloth to bar iron and precision tools. Their speed and convenience enabled even isolated communities to stay au fait with the latest fashions in everything from clothes to houses.

Hired coaches with their own livery and colours carried freight at a specific charge for a double mile (there and back). Coaches also spread the news of royal and political occasions and great events like Nelson's victories at Camperdown and Trafalgar and Wellington's triumph at Waterloo, the passengers shouting out the details as they went along. To mark the celebrations, the coaches were decorated with oak leaves and laurels, ribbons streaming from the reins and flowers tied to the harness.

MAIL COACHES

Mail coaches were also decked out on high days and holidays. At Christmas both vehicle and team were festooned with sprigs of holly and ribbons and the coachman and guard wore sprigs of mistletoe. Until the introduction of mail contracts in 1784, many coach services were withdrawn during the winter and the Mayday decorations symbolised the return to the regular routes. This was the only day when the strict timetable was allowed to lapse and at each town locals brought out sweets and cakes to the coachman, guard and passengers.

These decorated coaches sweeping into quiet towns would have been a thrilling sight to local people especially as the vehicles were already brightly painted, boasting names rather than numbers and with details of the stops displayed on the side. The bodies were made of wood and suffered constant jolting and stress, so they had to be well protected by paint to prevent water leaks and consequent rot.

The paintwork itself was highly varnished to minimise damage from the mud and stones thrown up by the wheels and horses' hooves. The finishes were superb because coach-builders would often apply up to fifty coats of paint and varnish. The coach body was suspended on 'thorough braces', leather straps designed to absorb the shock. Thanks to the constant nauseating swaying, travellers usually arrived at their destinations travel-sick and exhausted. After 1750, coach design improved and teams of faster half-bred or thoroughbred horses were used. The roads too were far better maintained and all these factors made travelling quicker and more comfortable.

Stage coaches were heavy vehicles, pulled by four to six horses and travelled at a steady 5 miles an hour. Inside were two cushioned seats, taking three people each side. Coaches could also carry up to 14 outside passengers, who travelled more cheaply, either in the luggage basket, which was slung between the back wheels, or on the roof.

THE FIRST MAIL COACH

In 1784, John Palmer, a Bath theatre proprietor, with the help of the Prime Minister, William Pitt the Younger, forced a reluctant Post Office to carry the Royal Mail by coach to and from London. The first mail coach left the Rummer Tavern in Bristol at 4 p.m. on August 2nd, 1784 and arrived in London at The Swan with Two Necks Tavern well before 8 o'clock the following morning. It had travelled 119 miles in under 16 hours. This earned Palmer the position of Postmaster General. Carrying the mail by coach ended the era of post boys who had a bad reputation for being drunk, unreliable and often in league with highwaymen. Mail robbery was so widespread that the Post Office itself advised those sending money or negotiable documents to cut them in half and send them by instalments. With the advent of the mail coaches, the menace of highwaymen disappeared because armed guards travelled with the coaches.

The Royal Mail coaches had a livery of deep maroon and black with red wheels. They were fitted with large lamps because they travelled at night and carried the Royal coat of arms on the door. The number of the coach was on the guard's seat at the back while the monarch's initials, GR were on the side nearest the front of the coach.

These mail coaches were built at the Millbank yard, Westminster, by Vidler, the junior partner of a man named Besant, who received the first contracts for mail coaches in 1787. Vidler made a considerable fortune because, rather than selling the coaches, he simply hired them to the contractors who ran the post routes, on a mileage basis. He had 27 coaches, each covering between 50 and 600 miles a week.

The coaches were driven hard and often needed repairs or replacement, but there was still a healthy profit to be made. The principal coaches had names. The Diligence to Bristol was always the first to leave London. The Tally-Ho! linked London and Birmingham; the Comet ran to Southampton, and the Defiance to Manchester. These were four of the best-known of the hundreds of coaches travelling the length and breadth of Britain.

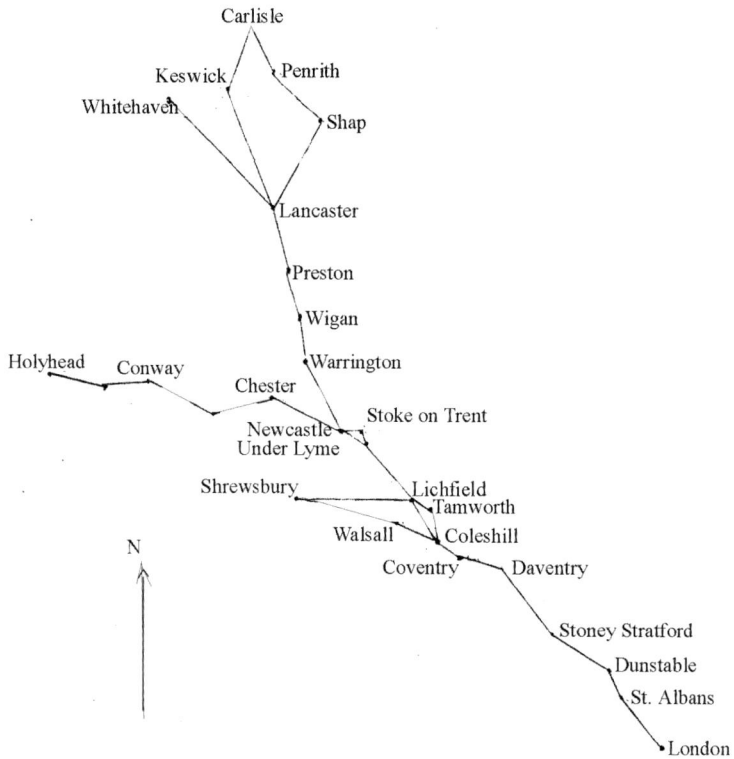

*Routes from London to Carlisle passing through Coleshill
(Compiled from Kitchen's "Travellers Guide through England and
Wales 1783")*

THE ROUTES

Taken from Coleshill Directory:
*"The Royal Mail coach to London from Liverpool calls at the
Swan hotel Coleshill every morning at half past ten; goes through*

Coventry, Dunchurch, Daventry, Towcester, Stony Stratford, Penny Stratford, Brickhill, Dunstable, St. Albans and Barnett.

The Alliance from Liverpool Calls at the same inn every evening at 8 and goes the same route as the Royal Mail.

The Accommodation, from Birmingham to Atherstone calls at the Swan every Monday, Thursday and Saturday evenings at 6. To Birmingham from Atherstone, the Accommodation calls at the Swan every Monday, Thursday and Saturday mornings at 9.

To Liverpool from London The Royal Mail calls at the Swan every morning at a quarter to eight (Monday excepted) through Lichfield, Rugeley, Stone, Newcastle. Congleton, Knutsford, Warrington and Prescot.

The Alliance from London calls at the Swan every morning at three and goes the same route as the Mail coach".

According to the directory, the Swan had two evening and three morning coaches.

TIMING THE COACHES

The time bills of 1797 show that the London to Liverpool Royal Mail coach delivered the time piece in Coleshill at 10.45am. The Royal Mail had to run punctually to a given timetable, an essential feature of Palmer's plan. As there was no universal Greenwich Mean Time then, everyone went by the local time, which was shown on a sundial. The parish church usually had one either on the building or mounted on a pillar in the churchyard. This meant that the far west was 20 minutes behind London.

To overcome this problem, each coach carried a time piece which could be regulated. This was secured in a strong case fitted with a lock and placed in a pouch worn over the guard's shoulders. On a long journey it had to be handed in to the postmaster at certain points to be checked or exchanged for another. At every check-point the postmaster had keys to unlock the case or to wind or regulate the timepiece and he had to sign for the instrument and enter its number on the time bill. John Dale was Coleshill's postmaster, a highly responsible position then, as he had to sign for the timepiece, one of only three officials on the London - Liverpool route to do so.

The time sheets had to be completed by the guard and returned to the office by the following mail. They were immediately scrutinised for any delays unaccounted for. Any contractor or guard at fault got a wigging by the next post from London. The guards were post office employees who wore scarlet tunics of military cut with gold lace frogging, nankeen breeches, white stockings and gold braided hats. They were issued with a uniform every year and carried blunderbusses, cutlasses and pistols to deter highwaymen. They also had a yard of tin, a long horn used to warn gatekeepers to open the gates as mail coaches did not pay tolls.

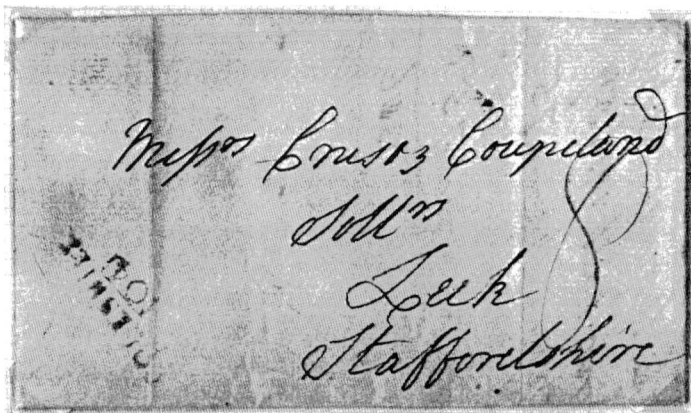

Letter dated October 7th 1818 from Charles B. Adderley of Hams Hall near Coleshill to Messrs Cross and Coupland, Solicitors, Leek, Staffordshire showing Coleshill postmark, mileage of 104 and charge mark of 8d

Guards were responsible for the safe keeping of the mail and getting it to its destination on time, regardless of difficulties. If a coach broke down, the guard would take one or both lead horses and deliver the mail bags on horseback alone, even in heavy blizzards. Ex-soldiers were often employed as guards because they were used to handling firearms and could stay awake. They were paid 10s.6d per week and also received regular tips from passengers plus sick benefit, retirement pensions and a contribution of 2 guineas towards funeral expenses.

The mailbags were put in the box under the guard's feet and this was kept locked at all times. At stops where the post office was off the main road, he had to carry the bags there after locking the box; a major difficulty in the dead of winter when his frozen fingers could hardly grip the key. The order to keep the box locked appeared on the sheets of instructions and any guard whose box was found unlocked had to forfeit a week's pay, while a repeat offence could mean dismissal.

A British Post Office in 1790

At sub-offices along the route, the guard would drop off the mail bags and pick up new ones from a forked stick, as the coach kept going at full speed, a practice which continued after the advent of railways. The trains also kept up the traditional method of time-keeping until time became universal.

The guard was trained to carry out roadside repairs on both coach and horses and he carried a tool kit and spares. The coaches had no brakes, just an iron shoe-skid which locked one wheel. At the top of a hill the guard had to apply this and remount, then jump down at the bottom of the hill to disengage it. Mail guards would travel between 40 and 60 miles, often on very little sleep, before they had to return with the opposite coach.

An act of Parliament in 1811 banned the discharging of firearms except in self defence, on pain of a £5 fine. Trigger-happy guards had been shooting at farm animals and stray dogs, while some had even killed or wounded escaped prisoners from the Napoleonic war. In certain cases, the Post Office had awarded the guards £5 for these feats of marksmanship, for saving the authorities the trouble and expense of capturing the escapees.

If the guard's summons on his horn to clear the way was ignored, the driver or owner of the offending vehicle was liable to a legal penalty. He could, however, write an apology which would be circulated to every post office. Whatever the problems encountered and regardless of weather, the mail had to get through on time, but this imposed a tough regime on everyone involved. The coachman, or whips as they were called, endured 50 miles of fast driving, often in atrocious conditions. The horses too were driven hard and only the best could stand the strain, while the guards carried heavy responsibilities throughout the entire journey and faced large fines for even a minor infringement.

EARLY TRAFFIC JAMS

Within the increasingly busy cities, however, even the fastest vehicles could barely maintain walking pace; the roads around the post office in London were so crowded, with up to 30 mail coaches lining up to disgorge their passengers and cargo, that regulations were passed forbidding hackney carriages to stand in the vicinity.

Hawkers were also banned from displaying their wares or loitering on the pavement, rules which apply today even though mail traffic no longer causes congestion. By the spring of 1785, mail coaches were running to Norwich, Leeds, Liverpool and Manchester. Within months, letters could be sent to Gloucester, Swansea, Birmingham, Oxford, Holyhead, Carlisle, Dover and Exeter and in 1786 the last important route, the Great North Road to Scotland, was opened.

In April 1801 new postal rates were introduced, starting at 3d for letters to be sent no more than 15 miles from any post office and increasing in proportion to the distance covered. In the same year, letters could be sent to America from the Birmingham Post Office on the first Wednesday in the month. Mail also went to Lisbon once a fortnight and to the West Indies every Wednesday.

From 1803 the mail coach fare from Birmingham to London travelling inside the coach was 2 guineas and 2 shillings, double the outside fare of 1 guinea and 1 shilling. Fares varied from route to route but mail coach prices were always higher than those for stagecoach travel. Mail coaches were a relatively small part of the coaching industry. By 1804 there were only 137 in England and Wales, though by 1834 this had risen to an all-time record of 261. At the same time there were 3000 stagecoaches, so mail coaches accounted for only 8% of all coaches used for public transport.

By 1827 services had increased on the new Lichfield to Birmingham road with 20 coaches a day bowling along at 10 miles an hour. The children's rhyme *"Ride a cock horse to Banbury Cross"* comes from the addition of a draught horse to help the team pull the coach up steep hills, like the one at Banbury cross-roads. Stage coach horses were changed after 10 or 15 miles; the faster mail coach teams after just 6 or 8. Between 1800-1830, over 1000 vehicles left London each day, using altogether 4000 horses, with hundreds more waiting all over the country to relieve them. On the Coleshill route, horses were changed at Barnet, The Black Bull in St. Albans, Dunstable, Little Brickhill, just outside Daventry at the Wheatsheaf Posting and Excise office, The Kings Head, Coventry and Stonebridge. The teams could be changed in a minute and a half. By the late 18th century, only the mail coaches called at the Swan in Coleshill and all passenger coaches were re-routed via Birmingham, a major blow to the local economy.

CHAPTER 4

THE COMING OF THE CANALS AND RAILWAYS.

Although the stagecoach routes through Coleshill were becoming less important by the end of the 18th century, thanks to the development of the Birmingham routes, it was the Industrial Revolution with its canals and railways which sounded the death knell of coaching. The railways in this area were built close to Coleshill town, the canals beyond the parish boundary to the north.

THE CANALS

The Birmingham and Fazeley canal through Curdworth, three miles north of Coleshill, was opened in 1789. Its construction created a bitter rivalry between Birmingham and Coventry, in which Coleshill played an historic role.

1768   The race for supremacy was on in the West Midlands. The businessmen of Coventry wanted to link their city to the local coalfields before Birmingham did the same. Both cities had Acts granted for a new canal and both hired James Brindley as engineer. The Coventry Canal would run from the Grand Trunk Canal (now the Trent and Mersey Canal) at Fradley, past Fazeley, Tamworth, Atherstone and Nuneaton to a basin in the centre of Coventry.

1769   Another group of businessmen, this time in Oxford, wanted to build a canal which would link their city to the Coventry Canal and the rest of the existing waterways network. Oxford on the River Thames and the Coventry Canal were to be the final pieces in Brindley's 'Grand Cross' jigsaw which was to link the four great rivers of England; the Mersey, Trent, Severn and Thames. The Oxford Canal was to join the Coventry Canal some way north of Coventry - which seems strange when Oxford is a long way south of Coventry!

The Quayside, Curdworth

42

However, this was in the days before embankments and cuttings and Brindley had to wind his way around the contours of the land. In fact, the Oxford Canal is probably the most convoluted in Britain.

1771 The money raised for the building of the Coventry Canal ran out before half the stretch was finished. The only completed part ran from Coventry to Atherstone, a long way short of Fradley on the Trent and Mersey Canal. However, this was well within range of the many coal mines to the north of Coventry. By this time the company had sacked their engineer, James Brindley. For seven years the route stood isolated. Meanwhile, their local rival, the Birmingham Canal, had long since been completed and was highly successful.

1778 The Oxford canal was open for 63 miles, running from the Coventry Canal at Longford to Banbury. Connecting the two canals proved difficult as the two companies argued over water losses and the exact meeting place. For a while the two routes actually ran side by side for several miles unconnected but eventually it was agreed to make a junction at Hawkesbury near Exhall.

   For the owners of the Oxford Canal, it was vital that the Coventry Canal should join the main canal network at Fradley. Unfortunately there was still not enough money available to complete it, so the two canals were left unfinished, both only half built, connecting to nothing in particular apart from each other.

1781 Despite their financial problems, the Coventry Canal Company still hoped to 'invade' the Black Country coal fields. The Birmingham Canal already ran into the prosperous areas around West Bromwich and Wednesbury but they had no outlet to the east. The Coventry Canal Company proposed to build a route from their canal to Wednesbury, just north of Birmingham. They got full backing from both the Trent and Mersey Canal and the Oxford Canal as both saw it as an opportunity to complete the missing link between Fradley and Atherstone.

1782 At a meeting in Coleshill, chosen because it was situated between Birmingham and Coventry, the project's supporters agreed that the new line would be known as the Birmingham and Fazeley Canal and would run east from Wednesbury to Fazeley. The Coventry Canal agreed to construct a link between their current terminus at Atherstone and the terminus of the new Birmingham and Fazeley. The Trent and Mersey Canal and new Birmingham and Fazeley Company agreed to complete the original Coventry route and meet at a point half way between Fazeley and Fradley. This amazingly friendly, multi-company partnership, an incredibly rare event, was known as 'The Coleshill Agreement'. However the Birmingham Canal Company were not about to let anybody sneak into their territory and steal their coal! They bitterly opposed the whole scheme and arguments continued for several years.

1784 Parliament entered the fray and eventually the Birmingham Canal won the day. The Government gave them permission to buy out the Birmingham and Fazeley Company and build a canal from the centre of Birmingham to Fazeley. They kept up the Coleshill agreement and the final parts of the Coventry Canal were built, although the Coventry Company, perhaps bitter at losing the battle, had to be pushed into completing their short stretch between Atherstone and Fazeley.

1788 With this canal almost finished and a link with Birmingham established, along with the stretch linking the Oxford Canal with the Thames, the Coventry Basin was extended, taking on the Y-shaped form it retains today.

1790 The Coleshill Agreement was completed when the final part of the Coventry Canal was opened. This allowed waterborne traffic to travel from Birmingham to London for the first time and meant the completion of Brindley's 'Grand Cross', 18 years after his death. Curdworth Quay became an important stop on the canal and according to old prints, it had a lock keeper's house and storage facilities with stabling for horses. From 1789 onwards, all Coleshill's coal came by road from Curdworth Quay.

THE RAILWAYS

Although railways were becoming important nationally in the last years of the Georgian times, none was built near Coleshill until after the end of the era. The Hampton line which linked Derby and the north with London and came through Whitacre, two miles east of Coleshill, did not open until 1839. The first Coleshill station was built a mile outside the town beside Maxstoke Lane. The line through Water Orton, two miles north of Coleshill, was opened a year later, in 1840. It was time to bid farewell to the stagecoach.

CHAPTER 5

THE GEORGIAN FAMILIES OF COLESHILL

Although the Civic Society archives contain many more records of people living in Coleshill in Georgian times, we have selected a few of the best-known families who retain a connection with Coleshill, or whose names are still commemorated in some way.

THE BARKERS

Six generations of Barkers, fathers and sons, practised medicine in Coleshill for almost 200 years, from 1698 to 1884. They lived, at least latterly, in Devereux House opposite the church where they are commemorated by a stained glass window in the Lady Chapel and a family vault outside, below the window. John Barker was both the town's doctor and a prolific author, writing not only on medical matters but also on high philosophy.

The Barkers' Family Tree (simplified)

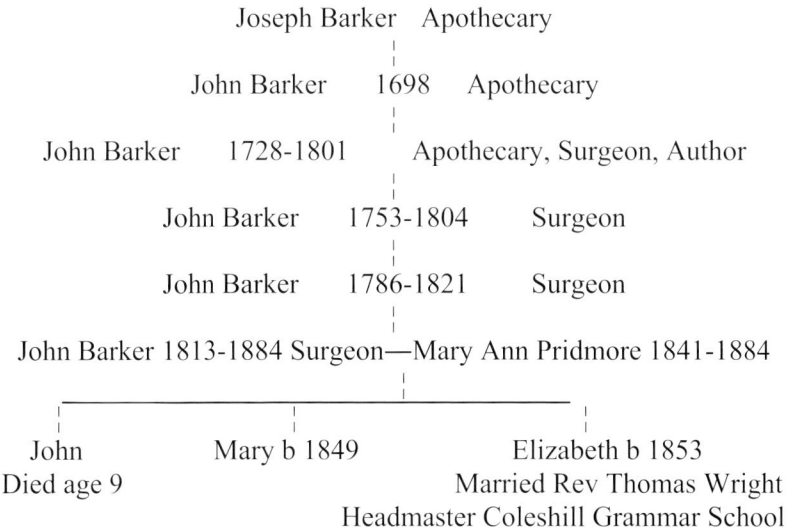

Joseph Barker   Apothecary

John Barker   1698   Apothecary

John Barker   1728-1801   Apothecary, Surgeon, Author

John Barker   1753-1804   Surgeon

John Barker   1786-1821   Surgeon

John Barker 1813-1884 Surgeon—Mary Ann Pridmore 1841-1884

John	Mary b 1849	Elizabeth b 1853
Died age 9		Married Rev Thomas Wright
		Headmaster Coleshill Grammar School

The last generation of Barkers died in the 1880's. They had married into the Pridmore and Wright families, the Pridmores living in Coleshill until recent years.

> *To the glory of God and in memory of his ancestors*
>
> *who for five generations from father to son*
>
> *practised as surgeons and apothecaries in Coleshill*
>
> *John Barker F.R.C.S. L.S.A. who also exercised*
>
> *the profession of medicine and surgery for 50 years*
>
> *in this town dedicated this window October 28th 1879*

Barker memorial window, Coleshill Parish Church

THE DIGBYS

Perspective drawing of old Coleshill Hall

The Digbys have been Lords of the Manor of Coleshill since 1495. In early Georgian times they lived in the old Coleshill Hall, a moated mansion near the River Cole on the road to Bacons End.

47

Hall Walk is one end of the green lane that runs over the M42 directly to the site of the old hall, where the remains of the moat are still visible as a dip in the ground.

The first Georgian Digby was William, 'the Good Lord Digby', a distinguished scholar and also M.P. for Warwickshire. When his grandson Edward, succeeded him in 1752, he moved the family seat to Sherborne Castle, where the clan (now called Wingfield-Digby) still lives. One of Edward's brothers, William, was Dean of Durham and Vicar of Coleshill, living in the enormous vicarage which is now Chantry House. His portrait was painted by Sir Joshua Reynolds.

Interior of Old Coleshill Hall

The Georgian Digbys were major local benefactors. They did much to renovate the Parish Church, built the first Market Hall in 1760 and founded the first girls' school in Coleshill in 1708.

THE FETHERSTON-DILKES

The Dilkes have owned the moated Maxstoke Castle since 1599. At the beginning of the Georgian period Ward Dilke was living there. He died in 1728 and was buried at Shustoke, passing on the estate to his son William II, (there had been an earlier William.) William III succeeded in 1749 and married Mary Fetherston-Leigh of Packwood House, the family subsequently changing its name to Fetherston-Dilke. William III became High Sheriff of Warwickshire in 1758. Four years later a serious fire destroyed a large part of the castle's west range. In 1785, William's son, William IV together with John, Lord Aylesford founded the archery club. 'The Woodmen of Arden', drawn mostly from the local gentry who had sent archers to the Hundred Years War. The Woodmen in their picturesque green tailcoats and including many descendants of the original families, still meet regularly at Forest Hall, Meriden for archery tournaments and social events.

Maxstoke Castle

William III, who had outlived his son, died in 1801, leaving William IV's widow Louisa in charge of the castle until her 6-year-old son, William V came of age. Louisa was a great innovator, totally refurbishing the castle, planting hundreds of trees and altering the approach to the castle from the Old Lodge by Blythe Bridge to its present entrance when the 'New Road' , Castle Lane, was built in 1815.

The family still live in Maxstoke Castle and continue the tradition of public service. Charles was High Sheriff of the County in 1974 and chairman of the County Council from 1978-80. His son Michael has also been High Sheriff in recent years.

THE DUGDALES

The Dugdale family has lived at Blythe Hall near Coleshill since 1625. The most famous, Sir William Dugdale, the author of 'Antiquities of Warwickshire' and a trusted aide of Charles I, was attaindered by Parliament during the Civil War and wrote most of his books while living quietly at Blythe during this period, between 1649 and 1660. After Charles II was crowned, Sir William was made a herald, part of the monarch's chivalric and genealogical secretariat, as a reward for his loyalty and scholarship, an honour passed down to his descendants, the last of whom, Sir John, his great grandson, died childless in 1749.

Copy of etching of Blythe Hall (1720), note Coleshill Church top left.

Blythe Hall, an elegant house beside the river, passed to John's sister Jane who had married Richard Geast from Handsworth in 1722. Their son, also Richard, married the heiress to the Merevale estate near Atherstone, Penelope Bate Stratford and in 1799 assumed by Royal Licence the surname and arms of Dugdale. Their son Dugdale Stratford Dugdale was born in 1773. The main branch of the family who were mainly local squires, minor politicians and active in local government, lived at Blythe until 1780 when they moved to Merevale Hall and over the next few decades, Blythe became the home of several generations of Dugdale widows until it was let to Mr Croxall of Shustoke House around 1825.

Between 1802 and 1830, Dugdale Stratford Dugdale was Tory MP for North Warwickshire and most of his descendants have also been active in public life, including his son William who stood for Parliament but was defeated by the Reverend Bracebridge Hemming of Mancetter in the first election after the Reform Bill in 1832. At the next election, William stood again and experienced a little local difficulty on the notoriously rowdy hustings at Coleshill, recording amusingly in his diary how a mob from Birmingham arrived, determined to rough up the Tory candidate.

"The Election took place for the first time at Coleshill; an immense number of persons of the lower order was marched in from Birmingham and Nuneaton in order to crush poor me - however in vain. By quietness and composure I at length obtained a hearing at the day of nomination, and parted upon very good terms with the assembled multitude."

The present owner, Sir William Dugdale, whose father received a baronetcy in 1936, spent most of his childhood at Merevale but moved into Blythe in 1953 and has lived there ever since. He is a former chairman of Severn Trent Water Authority and Aston Villa Football Club.

THE LEESONS

This long line of clockmakers started in Coleshill about 1830 when William Leeson arrived here as a young man in what was to become known at Clock Yard, (opposite the Tuckleys shop in High Street). By 1835 he was well established and renowned as the maker of church turret clocks. In 1860, he built the clock in Coleshill Parish Church, the same clock which keeps Coleshill on time to this day.

Both William's sons followed him as clockmakers. William moved to Manchester but Harry stayed on in Clock Yard, even setting up the Clock Inn at the front of the yard, apparently as a sideline.

Clock Yard 1910

Harry had six sons, three following their father into the clock trade, Charles 'Clocky' Leeson took over Clock Yard, Henry worked in Birmingham and Joseph moved to Sleaford, Lincolnshire. Of the other three sons, Thomas stayed in Coleshill acquiring property in Penns Lane and becoming successively a candlemaker, cycle maker and finally running a garage next to the Coach Hotel. Robert became an apprentice chemist to the Sumners before moving to Southampton and James the youngest became the town postman before and after the First World War.

James's son became a jobbing builder working from Penns Lane. He still lives there having married Mary Peach and thus uniting two of Coleshill's oldest families.

THE PEACH FAMILY

The Pearch family (later Peach) settled in the town at least three centuries ago. The earliest record is of Thomas Peach who died in Coleshill in 1720 and the family at first lived in Workhouse Lane, now Blythe Road.

The head of the family in the Georgian era was Richard (1754-1840) who worked as a cordwainer and married Elizabeth Cashmore of Coleshill in 1779. They had four children and their son Richard (1784-1848), also a cordwainer, married Elizabeth of Middleton. They had ten children.

Charles (1809-1875), the next head of the Peach family married twice. He moved into the cottage in Coventry Road, Coleshill (now called Peach Cottage) and had several occupations, including cordwainer and school master. The name Pearch was changed to Peach during his lifetime.

Peach Cottage, Coventry Road, Coleshill.

Charles had two sons, one a goldsmith and the other a silversmith, who both worked in the Birmingham Jewellery quarter.

Arthur (1844-1919), the silversmith, came back to the cottage when his father died. He married Caroline and they had six children.

Arthur (1877-1934), the elder, was apprenticed as a hairdresser in Stratford Upon Avon until he was struck down with influenza. His mother brought him home and he later opened a barbers's shop in the front room of the cottage, where he worked until his death. Arthur, known as Harry, was a popular man and is still remembered by a few older Coleshillians.

His only daughter Mary Peach was the last of a long line and married Jack Leeson in 1943. They had two daughters and four grandchildren.

Five generations of the family have been born in Peach Cottage, from Arthur in 1844 to Alex in 1973 and Richard's great great great great great granddaughter, Margaret still lives there.

THE PROSSERS

The Prossers were established in Coleshill by 1745. They appear in an early census as shopkeepers. Thomas (1794-1849) was a linen

The Prosser shop 1900

and woollen draper. One of his sons was farming Springfields Farm in about 1860. By 1880 J R Prosser and sons were established as grocers and corn merchants in No 84/86 High Street in the shop which is now Somerfield. One son, Charles (1872-1948), subsequently became a corn merchant operating mills at Blythe and Furnace End. In the next generation Dennis (1899-1982) became a farmer and corn merchant. Dennis's son Richard still farms locally.

In the early 1900's they achieved fame by cutting wheat in Maxstoke, threshing it on site in a portable winnowing machine, milling it at their Blythe Mill, baking the bread in their bakery behind their shop on the High Street. They then delivered it to Buckingham Palace by train from Coleshill Station, where it arrived within 24 hours of the wheat being cut in the field. Impossible today.

Blythe Mill

THE READINGS

Timothy Reading (1659-1730) lived in Bishops Tachbrook, near Warwick, as did his son Edward (1710-75) a carpenter, and his grandson Timothy (1749-94). His great grandson, Charles Reading (1781-1823) was married in Coleshill in 1804 and his descendents, variously spelt Reading or Redden, have lived here ever since.

Charles's son John Redden (b1813), one of the early railway workers, probably helped to build the Hampton line through Maxstoke which opened in 1839.

The cottages in Green Lane

Granny Gateley outside The Woodman in 1900

His son, Charles Reading (1841-89), also a railway worker, married Mary Ann, a nurse maid to the Digbys, who when Charles died, moved and kept a shop next to the Woodman pub, known as 'Granny Gateley's' (see photo on page 56 taken in 1901 at the relief of Mafeking). The shop sold everything from bootlaces to butter. Their son Ernest Reading, a bricklayer who lived in a cottage in Green Lane, was married twice and had eleven children. One of his children, Tony, still lives in Coleshill, as does Tony's cousin Mrs Madge Smith.

THE SUMNERS

In 1820 William Sumner, then aged 24, bought a grocery and druggist shop in the Bull Ring, Birmingham and in 1830 set up in Coleshill, in what is still a chemist shop, at 98 High Street.
The entry in Pigot's of 1835 reads :-
"Grocers and Tea Dealers Sumner, Wm. (also chemist and druggist), Coleshill".

"Colehaven," Sumner Road, Coleshill

TEA WAREHOUSE & DISPENSARY,
COLESHILL.

THE ALTERATIONS we have recently made have enabled us to devote the premises added entirely to the DRUG and DISPENSING DEPARTMENT, under the care of the manager, and a qualified assistant. We are now enable to pay the greatest attention to all PHYSICIANS' PRESCRIPTIONS and FAMILY RECEIPTS that may be entrusted to us, and to assure our customers that none but the Purest Chemical Drugs that can be obtained will be used in their preparation.

GENUINE PATENT MEDICINES. All kinds of MEDICAL APPLIANCES either in stock or obtained at the shortest notice. HORSE and CATTLE MEDICINES.

JNO. SUMNER,
COLESHILL AND BIRMINGHAM.

Advertisement from Coleshill Chronicle of 1878

A very early Typhoo Tea advertisement

From these small beginnings the business flourished and was passed from father to son, but they did not make their fortune until 1903 when they marketed the tea Typhoo Tipps as a health product. It caught the public imagination and the business took off. For many years the family lived at Blythe Cottage, now 'St Andrews', in Blythe Road, Coleshill and in 1930 John Sumner established the Colehaven Trust which built the almshouses in Sumner Road to benefit *"well-bred ladies of blameless character who found themselves in reduced circumstances"*. The quaint rows of cottages are still used as almshouses today, part of the national Elizabeth Finn Trust.

THE TUCKLEYS

The Tuckleys are an ancient family, probably originating from William de Tukkeley of Yardley (a mere 5 miles from Coleshill), in 1327. A mercer called Thomas Tuckley of Coleshill recorded a will in 1640 and a William Tuckley of Coleshill was buried there in 1721. From then on the male Tuckley line stretched unbroken in the town for 300 years until Thomas Tuckley, the present Miss Tuckley's father, died in 1944.

The Tuckleys seem to have been prosperous tradesmen and craftsmen for several centuries and are recorded as, successively:-

1640   Mercers (silk textile or small wares sellers)
1734   Nailmakers
1750   Braziers and Tinsmiths
1800   Ironmongers
1900   Ironmongers and Oil Merchants

The Tuckley Family Tree (simplified)

Wm de Tukkley of Yardley	1327		
Thomas Tuckley	1640	Mercer	Coleshill
John Tuckley	1724	Baker	Coleshill
Thomas Tuckley	1718-1768	Brazier, Tinsmith	Coleshill
Thomas Tuckley	1765	Nailer	Coleshill
Thomas the Elder	1770-1860	Ironmonger	Coleshill
Thomas Junior	1799-1869	Ironmonger	Coleshill
John Todd	1849-1924	Ironmonger	Coleshill
Thomas Tuckley	1880-1944	Ironmonger	Coleshill
Joan Tuckley	1923-	Ironmonger	Coleshill

Joan Tuckley, JP, and her sister continued to run the famous old ironmongers shop at number 80, High Street until 1986, the last chapter of a remarkable record of one family remaining in a town for many hundreds of years.

CHAPTER 6

GEORGIAN HOUSES

INTRODUCTION

To many Coleshill appears a Georgian Town as within its historic core, the bulk of the older buildings are brick-built in a Georgian style. Walking along the High Street, you see very few earlier timber-framed buildings, or later Victorian ones and this array of Georgian buildings implies a period of prosperity for many of Coleshill's residents during the 18th and early 19th centuries.

During redevelopment by Meriden Rural District Council in the 1950s and '60s, great swathes of ancient buildings along Church Hill and the Lower High Street were swept away and replaced by modern town houses. Many of the surviving Georgian buildings are now listed, although, in most cases, the listing descriptions are based only on a roadside view of the buildings, thereby missing many important internal features and complexities.

These buildings were mostly poorly understood, hence the decision to study them as part of a wider appreciation of Georgian Coleshill. This study has already shown many of these buildings to be more complex, more interesting, and in several instance much older, than previously believed. Work on the buildings continues and this chapter represents very much an interim statement on their historical and architectural potential.

BACKGROUND

Old Red Sandstone was extensively used in the Coleshill area for local church building, but the prevailing medieval and early post-medieval building tradition in North Warwickshire was for timber-framing, particularly at the vernacular level. A range of timber-framed houses mostly dating from the 14th to 16th centuries survives in the villages around Coleshill. These include one or two buildings of cruck construction, an early, primitive method of timber framing, quite distinct from the more common box-framed timbering. Within Coleshill there are only two or three buildings whose timber-framing is clearly visible. These include no. 37, Lower High Street whose simple box framing with curved wind-braces probably dates it to the 14th century. The timbered first-floor jetty of no. 148, High Street is of later date, probably 15th century, while the elaborate, decorative timbering of the old Three Tuns (now the 'Golden Tandoori'), an impressive half-timbered inn with coach access, is probably 16th century. Pound Cottage lay just outside the medieval town at a small hamlet called the Heath End, and along with Sky Cottage at Maxstoke, is one of the few thatched cottages still surviving in the area. Thatch, particularly straw thatch, was cheap and locally available for roofing but as it was a considerable fire hazard, wooden shingles were more often used for the town's street frontages until pottery roof tiles became more generally affordable towards the end of the medieval period.

Timber-framing was the favourite construction method in Coleshill until the late 17th century and would have dominated the street scene from Cole End Bridge, up the hill to the southern end of the town just past the present junction with Parkfield Road. Most of these buildings would have been townhouses of reasonable quality occupying measured burgage plots originally laid out earlier in the medieval period. It is thought that poorer quality houses and hovels stood across the river at Cole End, and as squatter houses down towards Coleshill Heath.

At the end of the 17th century there was a nationwide boom in the use of brick for vernacular buildings with hundreds of small brick kilns springing up wherever natural materials and market demand coincided. Ancient field and farm names suggest at least one series of kilns in Coleshill on what was then open heathland along the southern borders of the parish, although there is little evidence yet for how long the kilns were in operation.

THE GEORGIAN BUILDINGS

The social hierarchy in Coleshill in the early 18th century, at the start of the Georgian period, was dominated by the Digby family, the vicar, and then the larger farmers, the latter being a mixture of freeholders and tenants. Not surprisingly it is amongst this group that the great Georgian rebuilding of Coleshill started. The Digbys had led the way with modernisation work on their old manor house situated off the road to Bacon's End during the 17th century.

Laburnum House

The first tranche of Georgian brick buildings in Coleshill is typified by a projecting brick 'band' between ground and first floor level. The best example of this and arguably Coleshill's finest Georgian building, is the Swan on the High Street at its junction with Church Hill. Its mock stone edge quoinings and elaborate moulded eaves cornices all point to the rebuilding of what was even then Coleshill's oldest and most renowned coaching inn on quite a grand scale. Other early Georgian buildings within the town include the Old Grammar School at the top of Church Hill and Laburnum House in Lower High Street. Just outside the old town, Wheely Moor Farm and Springfield Farm (page 64) on Coventry Road also typify this style of brick building.

On present evidence all these early buildings seem to have been built from scratch, although most replaced earlier structures. However, this was not always the case amongst those constructed later in the 18th century when existing buildings were often given a 'facelift' by simply encasing and, in some cases extending, them in brick. The most basic form of brick 'modernisation' of an older

63

Springfield Farm

building was simply to remove the old wattle and daub infill between the timber framing and replace it with brick. A clear example of this is No. 37 Lower High Street where the narrow width of the bricks used indicates that this was done at an early date, either in the late 17th or early 18th century. The extension of this was to encase the outside of the building, or sometimes just the frontage itself, with brick, adding new windows and doors. Internally, there was also usually a re-fit sometimes altering floor/ceiling levels or constructing new corridors and fireplaces. When finished, such houses appeared to have been totally re-built, apart from perhaps the odd bit of timber-framing still left exposed in a side gable.

A cheaper form of this was simply to render the outside of a timber-framed building, as for example No. 148 High Street or the old Three Tuns Inn (now the Golden Tandoori). In the former case the overall shape of the building and its projecting first floor gable jetty rather give the game away. The rendering of the Three Tuns has been stripped away in recent decades to reveal once again the building's elaborate decorative timbering. So why did this great Georgian rebuilding take place? There are probably two reasons. Firstly house design was changing. 17th century buildings tended to have low ceilings, small windows and open 'inglenook' fireplaces, with the more important internal rooms wood heavily panelled. Visitors to the newly constructed Swan Inn, for example, would have found brighter airier rooms with high ceilings, larger sash windows and smaller, more formalised fireplaces with timber or marble over-mantles, etc. Older buildings within the town would have appeared distinctly darker and more cramped by comparison.

The second reason, and one with particular resonance today, is that amongst the almost claustrophobic social hierarchy typical of small market towns of this period, successful people were keen to show off their growing prosperity by modernising their properties. Most of the rebuilding took place in the mid-Georgian period, between 1740 and 1780, triggered by continuing agricultural prosperity and the modest growth of coaching traffic. Another important factor was the major improvement in the local road network through turnpiking. The poor state of the roads across much of England had, for centuries, been a major impediment to travel and trade. Potentially, bricks were widely available across England during the 17th century, but unless they were produced locally, the sheer cost of transporting them to places like Coleshill would have made them prohibitively expensive for all but the richest.

Devereux House and Old Bank House

In 1743 the road from Stonebridge across Coleshill Heath to Bacons End was turnpiked, followed in 1759 by the Chester Road, and in 1761 by the road east of Coleshill to Atherstone and Nuneaton. These improved roads, although tolled, made Coleshill more accessible to coaches and wagons, reducing the cost of bringing in building materials and boosting the rebuilding programme.

Some of the town's most impressive Georgian buildings were constructed along Church Hill. Unfortunately Meriden Rural District Council demolished those on the south side in the 1960s but of those on the north side, Devereux House and Old Bank House are architecturally the best. (page 65) Old Bank House is, in ground plan, a relatively small house, with an impressive Doric style porchway leading into a central hallway dividing two front rooms and two back

Church Hill, south side. Mrs Pridmore's House with 'White Lion Inn' to right.

rooms. The front rooms have projecting window bays, mirrored on both first and second floors, a feature unique within the town. During the 18th century many of the large houses had live-in servant accommodation built into their design, often with separate backstairs and other services. In the case of Old Bank House, the gap between it and Devereux House was infilled to act as a housekeeper's cottage with ground floor access into the main dining room at the front and also into the kitchen at the rear.

Some of the other larger properties included a second floor intended for servant accommodation, usually with separate stairway access down to the kitchen and other domestic buildings.

COLESHILL HOUSE CASE STUDY

Coleshill House, no. 141 High Street, is an excellent example of this and is also one of the most intriguing Georgian buildings in the town. For many years the ground floor has contained the town library, while the upper two floors have provided accommodation for the Digby family, lords of the manor, during their visits to the town. Along with its housekeeper's cottage alongside, the house's relatively unspoilt interior makes it one of Coleshill's most important surviving Georgian buildings.

Coleshill House

Other key features include a walled kitchen yard, coach-house, formal gardens and separate kitchen garden. The house itself consists of two parallel rectangular units of slightly different date, as demonstrated by two quite distinctive architectural styles and different brick sizes. These differences in style are also evident in internal features including decorative door frames, fireplaces or window fittings.

The back unit is the earlier; two stories high and with an east facing 'frontage' of three bays. The first floor has three sash windows, each with wooden glazing bars dividing it into twelve rectangular lights. The doorway is mid-late 18th century, of square relief columns surmounted by a dentilated pediment. Either side of the door are windows, the southern one appears to have been enlarged from the original and is now of twenty lights. The other is an early 20th century replacement forming a bayed French window.

The doorway in particular looks out of place here as its size and detail suggests a formal 'front door' but in this case it opens out into the garden. The rendering that covers the outside of the building makes it impossible at present say whether this doorway was part of the original construction or whether it was inserted when the house was extended to the front. The stairs to the first floor are in the hallway of this part of the building and face the street rather than this back doorway.

The front of the building, facing onto the High Street, was probably constructed towards the end of the 18th century, and is now almost fully rendered. It is of three storeys separated by protruding brick bands. The second floor is of reduced proportions but rises to a plain coped parapet also with a protruding parapet band. The frontage is divided by sash windows into five bays each with slightly wider central lights. On the ground floor the central bay is occupied by a rather grand porch in the Roman Doric style with fluted columns, triglyphs and moulded cornice hood. This porch opens into a central hallway with the two main rooms opening off either side. There are no stairs in this front section of the building. Access to the first floor is from the stairs at the rear.

To the north of this elegant frontage are two adjoining cottages that abut onto this building. Although both are also rendered, they are timber-framed and were clearly acquired when the new frontage to Coleshill House was being built because access to the second floor of the main house was created via the first cottage, while the rear of both cottages was used to create the walled kitchen yard with its sculleries, wash-houses and other domestic offices. Both cottages had their frontages rendered to match that of Coleshill House itself, but the rear of the properties shows 18th century brick re-facing. It seems likely that they were renovated during the building of the second, roadside, phase of Coleshill House in the late 18th century, when they were being 'planed in' to the expansion of the main house as domestic support units.

To the south of Coleshill House a modern wall and pair of double gates give access to the coach yard with its adjoining coach house and stables. The gardens are large with the section behind the coach house fenced off by walls and hedges as a kitchen garden to the main house. Coleshill House was therefore a large and prestigious property, matched only perhaps by No 1 Lower High Street and, within the town itself, only exceeded by its immediate neighbour, Coleshill Vicarage (now Chantry House). Like the vicarage, it was a Digby property (during much of the Georgian period the Digby family held the ecclesiastical living in Coleshill), and may even have served as the dower house, although the necessary research has not yet been done to prove this theory.

Unusually for Coleshill, the vicarage was built well back from the street and the original two storey Coleshill House was also set back from the roadside. Chantry House is the largest Georgian residence in Coleshill and stands in extensive grounds. It was probably planned and built across the site of several earlier plots. The main five-bay block is mid-Georgian, of three storeys with a double-glazed entrance doorway beneath a semi-circular Tuscan portico. The sash windows each have segmental heads, raised keystones, and giant angle pilasters. The contemporary with this is a two storey, single bay domestic block.

SUMMARY AND FUTURE WORK

Although research on the Georgian buildings of Coleshill is still incomplete with many still to be inspected, it has at least revealed that behind the Georgian brick frontages of the High Street, many, perhaps most, of these houses have earlier, timber-framed, cores. Unfortunately almost all the old buildings in Lower High Street were demolished in the 1960s without any record being made of them, but photographs taken by Eric Miller and others of the demolition work also show timbered interiors. This method of modernisation was understandably popular because it was cheaper and probably speedier than a complete re-build. Elsewhere in North Warwickshire, such as Kingsbury, 1950s PRC properties are currently having their original concrete panelled exteriors rebuilt in brick, making them look to all intents and purposes like new buildings.

Clearly when more Georgian buildings have been inspected a fuller picture will emerge. Wherever old deeds survive for these buildings, it may eventually be possible to discover who these 18th century rebuilders were and what their socio-economic role was within Coleshill. Finally, thanks are due to the many owners who have allowed members of the team access to their homes and properties, to explore in roof spaces, cellars and outhouses.

CHAPTER 7

THE INNS OF GEORGIAN COLESHILL

Of the 22 inns said to exist in Georgian times, 19 have been verified and their locations listed on the adjoining map. (The three inns for which no location is recorded are the Crowne, recorded 1706-1716, the Dog 1801-1806, and the Yeoman). Many were probably little more than small one-roomed ale houses with the landlord holding an additional job to swell the family coffers. However 11 are listed as having stabling, so must have had courtyards as well. Of the nine pubs and hotels in business today, eight were here in Georgian times (the exception being the Norton Arms), so a guided trail of Coleshill's Georgian inns would take in almost every pub in the town.

The commentary on the inns which follows is geographically arranged north to south with the reference letters from the map. All Eric Miller's photographs appear in 'Coleshill Remembered'.

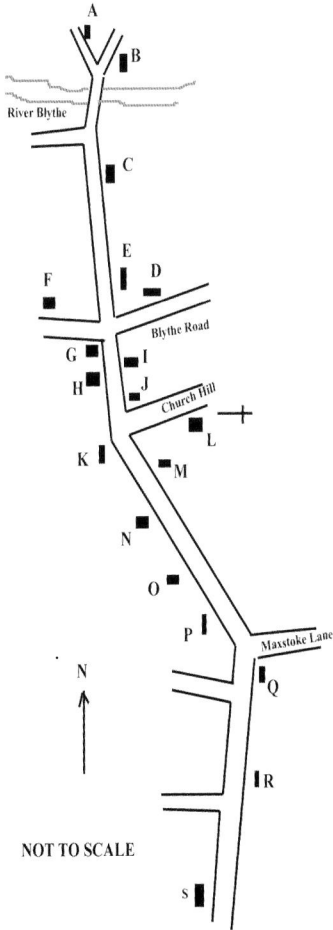

KEY	NAME	#	Secondary Occupation
A	Kings Head		Printer
B	Wheatsheaf		
C	3 Horse Shoes	#	
D	Workhouse Inn		Bricklayer
E	Lamb Inn	#	Plumber
F	Bell Inn	#	
G	Green Man	#	
H	Angel Inn	#	
I	Clock Inn		Watch Maker
J	Star Inn*	#	Hair Dresser
K	Swan	#	
L	White Lion	##	
M	3 Tuns Hotel	#	Sawyer
N	Beerhouse (Corbett)		Tailer
O	Coach & Horses	#	
P	Beerhouse (Gibbon)		Spinner
Q	Red Lion		
R	White Horse		Builder
S	George & Dragon	#	

\# =An Inn with Stables present
\#\# =Stables and a Gighouse
* =The full name of the Star Inn was
'The Star Inn and Posting House'

NOT TO SCALE

Sketch showing position of Georgian Inns in Coleshill

72

King's or Queen's Head with Wheatsheaf in background.

KING'S HEAD. (A)
Lichfield Road:

Appears to have changed its name to the Queen's Head possibly in Victorian times. It closed for business just before the 1914-18 war and was divided up into flats before being demolished in 1962.

WHEATSHEAF. (B)
Next to Coleshill Bridge.

Still open. It was known as the Bulkhead in 1817. Records exist from 1803 but parts of the building are reputed to be timber-framed and could be of an earlier date. It has recently changed its name to the Harvester.

THREE HORSESHOES. (C)
23 High Street.

According to records in Warwick CRO going back to 1767, *"Langley and his wife Mary sold the property to Thomas Cooke*

73

of Coleshill, coachman to the Liverpool Mail" in 1820. By 1850 it had a malt house and was occupied by a maltster. A well and pump in the yard are also mentioned. It remained an inn until the 1920s when it was divided into three dwellings, and the yard with two cottages became known as Shoes Yard. It was demolished in the 1960s.

THE WORKHOUSE INN. (D)
Blythe Road.

Presumably adjoined the Workhouse, but no record of it was found. This part of Blythe Road was known as Workhouse Lane.

THE LAMB INN. (E)
Lower High Street.

Situated below the crossroads on the east side, records start in 1806 and continue in Kelly's and Cope's Directories until 1940. It was demolished in the late 1960's.

THE BELL INN. (F)
Birmingham Road.

Still open. It was held by the Wheeldon family for 95 years from 1801-1896, and then by the Hextall family for a further 50 years until the 1940's. When Jim Childs bought it in the late 40's it was brewing its own beer. He kept it until 1971.

THE GREEN MAN. (G)
68 High Street.

Still open. Records exist from 1801 and the building is probably little altered since then. It had a meeting room and played a considerable part in the social life of the town. An old poster found in the pub and now in our archives advertises an 1811 production.

THEATRE, COLESHILL

On WEDNESDAY Evening, July 3rd, 1811,
Will be Performed, the very Celebrated Tragedy of

JANE SHORE,
Or, the Unhappy Favorite.

Duke of Gloster, Mr. DODD.   Lord Hastings, Mr. COWAN.
Belmour, Mr. PHILLIMORE.   Catesby, Mr. FERGUSON.
Ratcliffe, Mr. JAMES.   Earl of Derby, Mr. J. FENTON.
Dumont, (alias Shore,) Mr. W. FENTON.
Alicia, Mrs. COWAN,   Jane Shore, Mrs. FENTON.

End of the Play, a Comic Song by Mr. Charles, and a Comic Song called "the Comick Doctor," by Mr. J. Fenton.

After which the Musical Play of

Inkle and Yarico,
Or, the Blessings of Liberty.

Inkle, Mr. COWAN.   Sir Christopher, Mr. DODD.
Medium, Mr. PHILLIMORE.   Campley, Mr. JAMES.
Runner, Mr. CHARLES.   Planter, Mr. FERGUSON.
Trudge, Mr. J. FENTON.
Yarico, Mrs. COWAN.   Narcissa, Miss BANNISTER.
Betty, Mrs. PHILLIMORE.   Wowski, Mrs. FENTON.

To conclude with
GOD SAVE THE KING,
in full Chorus.

Nights of Performing, this Week, Monday, Tuesday, Wednesday, and Friday.
PIT 2s.   GALLERY 1s.
Tickets to be had of Messrs. Pearson—at the Principal Inns, &c. &c.
Doors to be opened at Half-past Six o'Clock, and to begin at Half-past Seven.

Wood, Printer, Bookbinder, and Stationer, New Meeting-street, Birmingham.

"Coleshill Theatre 1811."

THE ANGEL. (H)
74/76 High Street.
(Page 26)

An ancient coaching inn which retains its stage coach entrance into a cobbled courtyard at the rear, although its stables have become a mews development. Records go back to 1675. It is a listed building but little is left of the original interiors.

THE CLOCK INN. (I)
High Street

Part of Clock Yard. This stood on the east side of the High Street opposite the Angel and was owned by the Leeson family, Coleshill's clock-makers (see chapter 5). This was probably just a one roomed alehouse which was operated as a sideline until about 1850. The whole area was rebuilt as shops in the 1960's.

THE STAR INN. (J)
High Street.

This stood at the corner of High Street and Church Hill, and has now been replaced by a bank. Outside it was the parish pump. Records exist from 1801 to 1894.

THE SWAN. (K)
High Street.
(Page 25)

Still open. The Swan was the premier coaching inn in Georgian days, the stop for the Royal Mail, and the assembly place for the court. Many famous travellers stopped here (see chapters 2 and 3). It belonged to the Digbys as their estate records show:

1763 New Buckets at the Swan inn 17s.8d

1764 Paid Wm Webster for repairing and improving the Swan inn £100. Paid one year's insurance to Sun Fire Office £1-1s-0.

1783 Paid John Cheshire in full for new building at the Swan £57-18s-0.

1796 Expenses at the Swan Inn: a meeting with farmers asking them to agree to sell grain at reduced price to their labourers 17s-6d.

Sadly, although it is a listed building with a wonderful Georgian frontage, there is little left of its Georgian heritage in the interior, apart from the cellars.

THE WHITE LION. (L)
10-12, Church Hill.

This stood at the top of Church Hill near the Church, and was big enough to have both stabling and a gig-house. Records exist from 1819 to 1908. The building remained until the whole row was demolished in the 1960's.

The White Lion

THE THREE TUNS. (M)
107-109 High Street. (page76)

This listed building is still a licensed restaurant. Its delightful half-timbering dates it to the late 16th century. Its carriage entry still exists leading to what were once stable blocks at the back. In the mid 1900s it was a brewery and mineral water bottling establishment Dabbs and Nicholson's, whose green bottles are now collectors' items.

BEERHOUSE. (N)
128 High Street

No records exist but it could have been the inn later known as the White Swan or Little Swan, now Carter's electrical shop. This building, although not listed, appears to be Georgian in origin.

The Three Tuns

THE COACH AND HORSES. (O)
High Street.
(Page 27)
Still open. Known to have been built in the 19th century although there is little left of the original building except the old barn alongside. The wrought iron coaching arch appears to be a replacement. From 1894 to 1924, it belonged to the Farrin family who still live near Coleshill. Like the Swan, it boasted an assembly room and the Oddfellows met here in the 19th century. It also sported a bowling green at the rear beside the old brewhouse, now demolished, which became Coleshill's first cinema in 1920.

BEERHOUSE. (P)
Gibbon, 132, Coventry Road.
No records exist but it could be the forerunner of the Vine Inn which was later demolished to make way for the Coleshill Hotel.

78

THE RED LION. (Q)
11, Coventry Road.
Still open. Another old coaching inn dating from 1806, but with little recorded since. It recently changed its name to the Pepper Pot. Dare we hope that some future owner will change the name back again?

THE WHITE HORSE. (R)
Coventry Road.

Recorded as an inn from 1819 to 1940, it stood opposite the George and Dragon but was demolished to make way for Brendan Close in 1988.

THE GEORGE AND DRAGON. (S)
Coventry Road.

Still open. The original building dated back to 1801 and stood close to the road, as shown in the accompanying photograph taken in the 1900s. It was rebuilt, set back from the road in the 1930s.

Copy of old picture of the George and Dragon

CHAPTER 8

TRADES AND OCCUPATIONS

Georgian Coleshill was a self-sufficient town and although not quite in the same league as 20th century Birmingham, *"the city of a thousand trades"*, it nevertheless boasted over 150 different occupations despite being a community based on agriculture. These were a few of the area's major trades at the time:

MILLERS:

After farming, the most important trade was milling. Every stretch of waterway had a mill on it to produce flour for the all-important staple, bread. Coleshill had two water mills; the Town Mill on the River Cole at the bottom of the hill and Forge Mill on the River Tame. There was also a windmill in Parkfield near farm buildings belonging to Windmill Farm behind what is now Park Cottage on Birmingham Road.

The Town Mill was probably owned by the Digby Family who paid for repairs. It was an 18th century brick building, built on the site of an earlier mill, with an adjoining mill house. The waterwheel, mounted internally, was heavily used and often had to be repaired. In 1765 new flood gates were put in and repairs a year later cost £280-18-6, a huge sum in those days. The Manorial Court of William, Lord Digby in 1728 ensured that the Town Mill had plenty of water, ordering that *"Every person who shall stop the water running from Cripers Well to Eaves Spring or Colemeadow shall for every such offence forfeit to the Lord of this Manor a fine of 5 shillings."* The mills were usually run by families like the Louds and the Messengers. William Loud ran the Town Mill in 1793 but by 1828 it had passed to John Messenger whose family remained in charge of it until 1872.

Forge Mill was marked on Beighton's map of 1725 but its earlier history is unknown. There was possibly one mill with two pairs of stones as it was often mentioned as Forge Mills. The Digbys' Coleshill estate accounts show them paying for work and repairs at Forge Mill. William Falconbridge was the miller there in 1770 when a pair of new French millstones was installed. In 1786 William Wilcox, a millwright, was paid £2-16-6 for work at 'Falconbridge Mill' (Forge Mill) while in 1797 the Rt. Hon. Edward, Earl of Digby leased the mill house, lands and appurtenances at Forge Mills

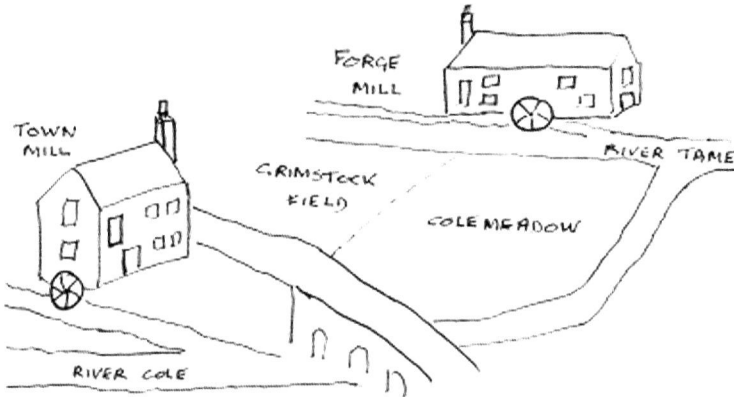

to William Penn of Hazelwell Mill in Kings Norton, a gun barrel borer, and Joseph Grice of Birmingham, a gunsmith. In 1800 Penn, Grice and John Dale of Coleshill, a mercer, leased the property for one year. In William, Lord Digby's manorial court of 1728, he insisted that his tenants maintain a reasonable pathway from Coleshill to the mill: *"Ye tenants or owners of the Lands in Colemeadow against Grimstock field shall sufficiently repair the footway leading from Coleshill to the Forge Mill or keep the same repaired on or before St. Andrews Day next or any persons making default shall for each his neglect shall forfeit to the Lord of this Manor in the Name of a pain [fine of] 10s."* Coleshill railway station was later built close to the mill and was originally named Forge Mills Station.

The two local water mills were financed by the Lord of the Manor, who would have charged a hefty sum to use them. Independent farmers would probably have been the last to have their grain milled so Coleshill's windmill would have provided them with a popular alternative. It was a post mill or a tower mill built of stone and brick, standing within three fields not owned by the Digby Family and mainly used by people who were not tenant farmers. It appears on John Snape's map of the town in 1783 so it was built before then. Among the men recorded as millers there are Robert Shuttleworth in 1828 and Francis Wood in 1835.

MOLE CATCHER:

Mole catchers were apparently few and far between and Coleshill's hailed from the neighbouring parish of Corley. In 1723, the town's parishioners drew up a 21-year agreement with John Gibson. He was to be paid yearly by the overseers of the poor out of the Poor Levy. Gibson must have been good at his job as in 1752 another agreement was drawn up, this time for 30 years. He was paid *"Ten pounds a year for the two first years and six pounds a year for the remainder of the said 30 years"*. In 1783 a new 21-year agreement was signed with John Gibson (who must have been an old man by now) or any of his sons who *"shall catch and clear all the lands being as lying in the parish of Coleshill of all the moles at and under"* for the sum of four guineas a year. It seems to have been a lucrative job in 1752

83

but paid less in 1783, perhaps because he had done his work so well that fewer moles were left by then. Also he would presumably use or sell the skins from the moles he caught.

TANNER AND CORDWAINER:

Coleshill had its own tannery down by the river Cole and many older residents will remember the remains of the building which lay behind St. Paul's School. It was owned by the Pridmores, a prominent Coleshill family. The tannery and the leather it produced gave rise to various other trades in the town, including that of cordwainer. There were 18 cordwainers or shoemakers listed in the 1811 census and 15 in 1821. According to the History of the Market Hall, a deed of 1791 says that on *"25th March 1791 Clement Hill cordwainer of Coleshill takes a mortage of £200 from Joseph Stretton of Coleshill (a shopkeeper and a dealer in earthenware) on the property".* The property was described as a *"messuage or tenement, stableyard and buildings in High Street".*

During restoration of the Old Market Hall, an archaeological dig found numerous leather cut-outs and broken pottery shards dating to the 17th and 18th centuries. A brick carving on the building bearing the legend *"T S 1793"* could belong to Joseph Stretton's son Thomas.

There are references to children being apprenticed to cordwainers: in 1794, John Linforth had William Watkins of Great Packington as his apprentice; in 1824, John Turpenny Junior apprenticed Thomas Savage for 7 years, agreeing to give him instruction only; his father had to feed and clothe him. After two years Thomas was paid 4s per week for the next two years and 6s from then on. In 1827, Edward Scoffain, aged 16 or thereabouts of Coleshill was apprenticed for the sum of £5 by his parents to Charles Barlow, cordwainer, until he was 21. In the same year William Eaves failed in his business of cordwainer and was unable to employ or maintain his apprentice.

BREECHES MAKER:

Leather Breeches Maker was another trade allied to the Tannery. In 1767 Richard Eaves was apprenticed to Thomas Golsall of Coleshill, a breeches maker and in the 1821 census a *"leather breeches manufacturer"* was listed. In 1827 Coleshill Parish Occasional Relief Book lists under July 9th that Thomas Haines was given 2.0 shillings to help him on his way back to London, he having come down to Coleshill to claim his settlement by apprenticeship with Tho. Godsal leather breeches maker.

SADDLER:

With a ready supply of leather and agriculture as the main local industry, saddlery was naturally an important occupation in the town. In 1793 Charles Twomlow was apprenticed to Thomas Forshaw of Coleshill, a saddler who in 1800 took another apprentice, 13-year-old Charles William until he was 21. Hannah Forshaw, named as a saddler in West's 1830 Directory and likewise in Pigot's Trade Directory, was presumably a descendant of Thomas Forshaw, carrying on the family trade. Thomas Eaves and Thomas Myring were also named as saddlers. More than 70 years later William Myring carried on a saddlery business at premises in Lower High Street and Coleshill boasted a saddler's shop until the 1960s.

FLAX SPINNER:

Flax spinning also took place in Coleshill. The Manorial Court of William Lord Digby of 1728 states: *"If hemp or flax was watered in any of the Lord's Rivers or his pools a fine of ten shillings was imposed"*. Flax was definitely grown locally, however, as in 1760 Thomas Smith was apprenticed for six years to John Mills of Coleshill, a flax draper, who later became a flax dresser and took on John Garret as his apprentice. A flax dresser is also listed in the 1811 census and a flax spinner a decade later.

CLOCKMAKER:

A clock and watch maker was an important personage in a town like Coleshill. In the 18th century the majority of clocks were found on the parish churches and for most of Coleshill's inhabitants, the church clock was the only means of telling the time, so it was essential that it kept good time and was wound regularly. In 1764, William Vale, a local clockmaker, agreed with the church wardens John Watts and Thomas Mills to *"repair the church clock of Coleshill for the sum of ten pounds"*. He also agreed to become bound to the wardens to *"do from time to time and at all times hereafter for and during his natural life at his own costs and charges being allowed and paid yearly and every year 15 shillings, well and sufficiently amend, repair and wind up the said Church Clock of Coleshill as often as the same shall need and require to be done and keep in as regular order as a good church clock ought to go"*.

The Digby Estate Accounts record that on Michaelmas 1765, William Vale was paid 3s for repairing a clock at Coleshall and in the same year he earned 1s 6d for cleaning clocks at Coleshall. There was obviously plenty of work around, as three clockmakers feature in the 1811 census. In 1828 R. Bannister and Charles Crosby were listed as clockmakers and in 1835 Thomas Hartshorn was named in the trade directories.
:

TAILOR

The tailoring trade was a thriving business and the six tailors recorded in the 1811 census had risen to 13 by 1831. The records show that in 1746, David Rathbone was apprenticed to David G. Walker of Coleshill, a tailor, while in 1793, Joseph Mumforde, 14, a poor child, was apprenticed to another tailor Edward Rhodes. Three years later another Coleshill tailor William Shelley asked for the discharge of his apprentice William Cotterill who was not capable of learning his trade. In 1803, Shelley took on William Wallbank aged 14 and a year later, 12-year-old Richard Cliffe, became an apprentice to William Eaves. Between 1828 and 1835 six tailors were listed in the various trade directories; William Eaves plus Edward Attridge, James and William Mallet, James Reppington and Thomas Prosser who by 1835 was also a draper.

BASKET MAKER:

Basket making was based on the supply of withies from the willow trees beside the River Blythe where willows still grow today. One basket maker in Coleshill was called Thomas Birch. Two were listed in the 1811 census and three in 1821.

BROOM AND BESOM MAKER:

The two trades of broom and besom making were carried on in Coleshill. In 1811 there were four people making besoms, five in 1821 but only one in 1831. In Pigot's Directory of 1828/29 and again in 1835, a Coleshill brush maker, William Haywood, is listed without detailing what kind of brushes he made.

BUILDER:

The building trade was busy during the Georgian period but mainly repairing or altering existing buildings. A few new buildings were erected, including the Market Cross, an arcade or arched structure Henry Lord Digby had built in 1766 for the use of the market. The Coleshill Estate accounts for that year state: *"Michaelmas 1766 Paid to Thomas Cheshire for building the Market Cross at Coleshill £63"* and on Michaelmas 1767: *"Paid Thomas Cheshire the remainder of his bill for building the Market Cross - £17"*. An inscription on this building read: *"Henticus Dux Digby hanc Porticum in usam huyas Emporia struxit Anno 1766"*. [Henry, Lord Digby built this arcade for the use of this market in the year 1766.] Thomas Cheshire was also paid 10s 6d on Lady Day 1722 for drawing a plan and giving an estimate for a new house at Coleshill Hall but this was not built in this period. In 1771 the Digby Estate paid £90 for a new barn at Gilson for Thomas Madely and £40-13-2 for a new granary for Joseph Underhill. Interestingly, both Madely and Underhill were tenants and they had to pay 5% towards the cost.

Four years later Thomas Jaques was paid £24 for building a granary and wagon house for which he agreed to pay 24s per annum. In 1778 William Chamberlayne was allowed £34-4-6 for digging a well, bricks and a pump, presumably at the Swan, where he was landlord. He was to repay the above amount at 5% interest.

The Swan apparently needed frequent alterations or improvements. In 1764, William Webster received £100 for repairing and improving the Swan Inn and in 1777 William Deebank, a mason, was paid £28-14-0 for work there. Six years later, John Cheshire was paid £57-18-0 for the New Building at the Swan, having already received £78-4-0 on account for this work. £1-8-2 was later paid out for a minor repair but in 1789 £10 was paid to Mr. Chamberlayne for yet more work at the Swan.

The mason William Deebank in 1769 earned £1-7-9 for work at Coleshall. In 1777, together with Thomas Linex, he repaired William Burnet's stable. In 1830 another William Deebank, a bricklayer and presumably descendant of the above mason, was carrying on the family business. In 1773 timber to raise the vicarage roof cost £30. Coleshill Bridge had to be repaired, first in 1784 which cost £21 and again a decade later. A mason's porter was listed in the 1811 census, possibly the forerunner of the hod carrier of today.

TILER:

A tiler is not listed in the census rolls but in 1775 Coleshall Estate paid several bills for new tiling on the stables at the Hall and when the vicarage roof was raised, it was probably tiled.

BRICK MAKER:

Besides masons and bricklayers there were also brick makers who used brick kilns on the edge of the heath to the south of Coleshill. On the Ordnance Survey one inch map, drawn up in 1820 but not published until 1834, there is a road called 'Brickhill Street' in this area and nearby, close to the Chester Road, is Brickfield Farm. From this evidence, it appears that the area between Stonebridge Road and Chester Road, south of Coleshill Heath Road was devoted to the making of bricks.

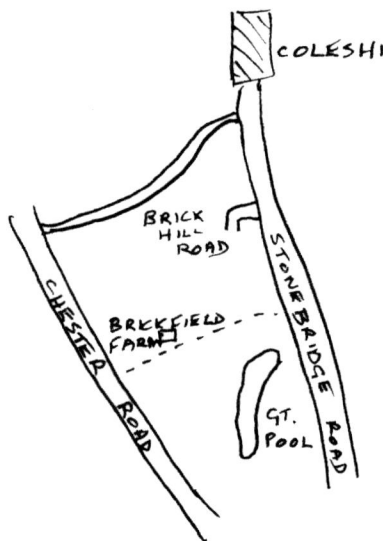

LIME MERCHANT:

Lime was in great demand by the building trade as it was used to modernise old buildings made of wood and plaster by concealing their timber work behind a cement (lime) rendering. In 1769 George Jennings was paid £10-10-0 for four loads of lime used in the repair of the barns at Coleshall and later received another £2-15-0 for lime used at Coleshall. In 1777 William Chamberlayne used lime in the repairs at the Swan Inn.

TOWN CRIER AND BAILIFF:

In 1804 Edward, Earl of Digby paid John Cashmore 10 shillings and 6 pence for one year's salary as town crier and bailiff. He was employed as bailiff to collect unpaid manorial fines (or amercements) imposed by the Court Leet, for not attending court or other similar offences, such as not cleaning out ditches or mending hedges etc. In this case the amount of the fines collected just covered the wages for the duties carried out viz; 10s 5d.

MALTSTER:

The maltster produced malt, a vital ingredient in brewing beer. The old Georgian Malthouse stood behind the houses on the east side of Lower High Street, facing north and close to where the telephone exchange is now. It was in existence in 1737. The two storey building was built of brick and timber with a lower floor providing:

90

"one large space, very low, about 30 yards long and six or seven yards wide. The floor of the upper storey was supported by massive oak beams, 15 inches square and 18 feet long and nine in number".

Upstairs there was a room used as a drying area. It was paved with large fireproof tiles, supported on iron bars and perforated to allow hot air from the furnace below to pass through. The furnace, which occupied nearly the whole area beneath the drying room, was square and resembled a large pillar arching out to the sides. There were two maltsters in Coleshill in 1811 but by 1831 this had risen to 7.

GLAZIER, PAINTER AND PLUMBER:

Glaziers, painters and plumbers worked in Coleshill at this time. The word plumber derives from the Latin word for lead, 'plumbum' and as all three trades were linked to lead in the Georgian era, a single person could be called a glazier, painter or plumber as he carried out all three jobs. Coleshill Hall Estate Accounts record a payment of £3-4-0 at Michaelmas 1763 to a plumber for work at Coleshall. Four years later the plumber was named as Edward Wright and was paid £3-0-8 possibly for glazing work at the Hall. Payments were also made to Wright in 1771, 1775 and 1776, the latter for work done at the Swan Inn totalling £13-3-0. There were three plumbers in 1811 and four in 1821. Later in West's Trade Directory two plumbers were listed; James Taverner and Richard Eaves.

BLACKSMITH:

We tend to think of the village blacksmith as a big and brawny man and most probably were but in 1781 Coleshill had a woman blacksmith. In that year Henry Nichols, aged 15, was apprenticed to Elizabeth Moore, a widow, to dwell with her and serve *"in the Art, Trade or Business of a Blacksmith"*. Elizabeth Moore *"shall and will teach and instruct or cause him to be well and sufficiently taught and instructed therein"*. Perhaps widow Moore was carrying on her late husband's work and needed the help of a poor boy.

PERRUQUE MAKER:

A perruque or peruke maker made and looked after the wigs, which played an important part of a gentleman's wardrobe in the 18th century. The wigs needed constant attention, providing regular work for the barbers who would dress them with pomatum ointment to keep the curls in place and powder them with rice starch. In 1703 John Jones of Coleshill, a perruque maker, and his wife Judith bought two *"dwelling houses with appurtenances"* in Coleshill. He was later referred to as a barber. In the 1811 census there were two peruke makers but in 1821 none was mentioned, although two barbers or haircutters were listed. This reflected the wig's decline in popularity in the 19th century when hair care became the job of the barber.

MILLINER AND MANTUA MAKER:

A milliner and mantua maker is mentioned in Coleshill in the Georgian Period. In 1818 Mary Keen, a poor child from Leamington Priors and Elizabeth Eden of Little Packington, were apprenticed to Sarah Payton, a milliner and mantua maker. Elizabeth was to be instructed "*in the Trade or mystery of Mantua making*". A mantua was a woman's loose gown worn open in front to show the underskirt and it appears that milliners and mantua makers represented the posh end of the dress-making business.

92

ROAD SURVEYOR:

A road surveyor, named John Valentine, was listed in the 1828/29 Pigot's Directory of Warwickshire under Coleshill and in the 1830 West Directory. He drew up a map of the parish in 1840, probably based on an existing map of the area but as a road surveyor he would have walked all the roads in the district and have known them well. A copy of his huge map hangs in the Old Market Hall.

SOLICITOR:

Two solicitors practised in Coleshill at different times in this period. Mr Lees, followed in 1771 by Mr. Palmer, acted as agents for the Digby Family who were not living locally. Mr. Palmer saw to the payment for work done at the Hall and was also involved in selling property including the White Lion on the south side of Church Hill, now demolished.

ROAD SWEEPER:

On market days a road sweeper was much in demand, as a byelaw passed at the Manorial Court of William Lord Digby in 1728 stated that *"Hugh Gardiner having the benefit of stalls near the Market Place shall Cleanse the Way thro the cross for people to pass to church on or before the fifth day of November next. And so keep the same weekly or forfeit to the Lord of his Manor for every neglect in the Name of a pain - Ten shillings".*

METAL WORKERS:

Metal work was a major occupation in Georgian Coleshill and tin workers, braziers, brass founders, blacksmiths, ironmongers and nailers are all mentioned in records of the time. The Tuckley family was involved in many of these trades until the latter part of the 20th century. (See Pigot's Directory, p.94.)

This list provides a sample of just a few of the trades found in Coleshill during the Georgian times. The extraordinary variety of occupations, ranging from alesellers to woodturners, is reminiscent of the nursery rhyme lines about *"The butcher, the baker, the candlestick maker"*. The long list featured many occupations in which women as well as men were well-represented and adds to the impression of Coleshill as a thriving and prosperous community during this period.

LIST OF TRADES IN GEORGIAN TIMES

Ale Seller
Army
Attorney
Auctioneer
Baker
Basket Maker
Besom Maker
Blacksmith
Book Seller
Brandy Merchant
Brass Founder
Brazier
Breeches Maker
Brewer
Bricklayer
Bricklayer's Labourer
Brick Maker
Brush Maker
Butcher
Cabinet Maker
Carpenter
Carrier
Chaise Driver
Charwoman
Cheese Factor
Chemist
Clergyman
Clock Maker
Clog Maker
Coach Guard
Coach Maker
Coachman
Coal Carrier

Collar Maker
Cooper
Cordwainer
Cow Dealer
Currier
Draper
Dealer Dealer in Pots
Doctor
Dress Maker
Druggist
Exciseman
Farmer
Farrier
Fire and Office Agents
Flax Dresser
Flax Spinner
Gardener
Gardener / Pig Killer
Gent's Servant
Glazier
Grocer / Tea Dealer
Groom
Harrier
Hatter / Hat Manufacturer
Hatter's Weaver
Hawker
Higler
Horse Breaker
Horse Dealer
Horse Keeper
Hostler
Household Servant
Huckster

LIST OF TRADES IN GEORGIAN COLESHILL

Inn Keeper
Ironmonger
Jersey Spinner
Jobbing Work
Joiner
Keysmith
Lawyer
Leather Breeches Maker
Letter Carrier
Linen & Woollen Drapers
Liquor Merchant
Mail Coachman Mail Guard
Maltster
Mantua Maker
Map Maker
Mason
Mason's Porter
Mercer
Miller
Milliner
Millwright
Musician
Nailer
Navy
Nursing
Oatmealman
Overseer of the Poor
Painter
Paper Maker
Park Keeper
Pedlar
Perfumery Warehouseman
Peruke Maker
Plumber
Porter
Post Master
Preacher
Printer
Professor of Music

Publican
Rag Gatherer
Rake Maker
Road Sweeper
Rope Maker
Rounds Joiner Saddler
Sawyer
School Master
School Master / Clergyman
School Mistress
Seamster
Seedsman
Sexton
Shoe Maker
Shop Keeper
Spinner
Spirit Merchant
Straw hat Maker
Stationer
Surgeon
Surveyor of Timber
Surveyor of Roads
Sword Blade Grinder
Tailor
Tallow Chandler
Tanner
Timber Merchant
Tin Shop / Tin Man
Turner & Chain Maker
Turnpike Roadsman
Veterinary Surgeon
Victualer
Waiter
Washer Woman
Watch Maker
Water Carrier
Weaver
Wheelwright
Wood Turner

NOBILITY, &c.—Continued.
Salmon Rev. George, M.A.
Shirley Charles, esq. Vicarage house
Swan Mrs. Naomi
Taverner Joseph, gent.
Tooth Richard, esq.
Towns Samuel, gent.
Wood Miss Sarah
Woods Miss Catherine
Woods Mrs. Mary
Wright Thomas, gent.
York Miss Ann

ACADEMIES & SCHOOLS.
FREE GRAMMAR SCHOOL, Rev. Geo.
 Salmon, classical master; Wm.
 Tite, commercial master
Hodgson Miss, (ladies' boarding)
Wharr Elizabeth & Mary (ladies'
 boarding and day)

ATTORNEYS.
Palmer Edward Fielding
Palmer Thomas

BAKERS & FLOUR DEALERS.
Harris William
Jackson William (& confectioner)

BASKET MAKERS.
Birch Thomas
Ward William

BLACKSMITHS.
Butler Joseph
Morris Thomas

**BOOKSELLER, STATIONER &
PRINTER.**
Tite Wm. (& stamp distributer &
 patent medicine and perfumery
 warehouse)

BOOT & SHOE MAKERS.
Butler Hannah
Dabbs Timothy
Daniel Joseph
Linforth John (& patten maker)
Peach Richard
Spencer George
Turnpenney John

BRAZIERS & TINMEN.
Jones David
Tuckley Thomas

BRICKLAYERS, &c.
Deebank William
Langley Edward
Morris Thomas
Slater Joseph

BUTCHERS.
Clarke Ann
Drakeford Arthur
Roobottom Thomas
Todd Anthony

CARPENTERS, &c.
Corbett William
Fletcher John
Heap John
Kendall Joseph
Reeves Charles, (& auctioneer and
 appraiser)
Shuttleworth Edward
Smith William

CORN MILLERS.
Holmes Joseph, FORGE MILL
Load James, Maxtoke
Messenger John, COLESHILL MILL
Messenger John, sen. Whitacre
Sheffield Thomas, BLYTH MILL
Shuttleworth Robert, Coleshill
Twamley Zachrh. Castle Bromwich

Watson Arthur, Furnace end
York Sarah, Kingshurst

FIRE, &c. OFFICE AGENTS.
BIRMINGHAM, John Dale
COUNTY, William Tite

GROCERS & TEA DEALERS.
Dale John
Newbold Richard
Richardson Thomas

INNS.
Coach & Horses (& excise officer)
 Thos. Burbidge   [Smith
Swan Hotel (& posting house) Saml.

LINEN & WOOLLEN DRAPERS
Dale John
Prosser Thomas
Ratheram Robert (& mercer)

MALTSTERS.
Burbidge Thomas
Burdett Richard Brearley
Burton William
Chamberlain William
Cotterill Joseph
Greathead John
Hartelow Thomas, Whitacre
Lane Edward
Thornley Chas. Marson hall, Sheldon
Todd Joseph, Whitacre
Ward Richard, Maxtoke hall
Weston John, Whitacre
Wright John, Minworth

**MILLINERS AND DRESS
MAKERS.**
Harris Ann
Newell Maria
Saunders Mary
Ward Sarah

NAIL MAKERS.
Tuckley Charles
Tuckley Thomas

**PAINTERS, PLUMBERS AND
GLAZIERS.**
Douce James
Eaves Richard
Taverner James

PAPER MAKERS.
Messenger Thomas, Whitacre
Smith Thomas

SADDLERS.
Eaves Thomas
Forshaw Hannah
Myring Thomas

**SHOPKEEPERS & DEALERS
IN SUNDRIES.**
Cox Esther
Devey William
Gutteridge Martin
Hobbey Richard
Kendall Joseph
Linforth Richard
Masters William

SURGEONS.
Barker and Owen
Davies John
Downing and Paterson

SURVEYORS.
Demolo John
Shuttleworth Edward (timber)
Valentine John (road)

TAILORS.
Attridge Edward
Eaves William
Mallett James
Mallett William

Prosser Thomas
Reppington James

TALLOW CHANDLERS.
Jefferys Joseph
Newbold Richard

TAVERNS & PUBLIC HOUSES.
Bell, Thomas Wheeldon
George & Dragon, William Debank
Green Man, Geo. Rodney Shuttleworth
Lamb, Ann Garratt
Red Lion, Edward Bates
Star, William Rathbone
Three Horse Shoes, Thos. Mammatt
Wheat Sheaf, George Turnpenny
White Horse, Thomas Morris

TURNERS.
Haywood Joseph
Moor Joseph (chair turner and
 spinning wheel maker)

WATCH & CLOCK MAKERS.
Bannister Richard
Crosby Charles

Miscellaneous.
Bee Thomas, hair cutter, &c.
Bint John, brandy merchant
Bowers Enoch, tanner
Hayward William, brush maker
Horton William, hat maker
Morgan John, excise officer
Reeves Thomas, wheelwright
Smallwood Chas. cooper & patten maker
Stretton Mary, rope, line, twine and bed
 sacking manufacturer
Stretton Thomas, currier
Stretton Thomas, druggist
Swinnerton Hester, straw hat maker
Ward John, millwright

COACHES.
To LONDON, the *Royal Mail* (from Liverpool) calls at the Swan Hotel, every morning at half-past ten; goes through Coventry, Dunchurch, Daventry, Towcester, Stony Stratford, Fenny Stratford, Brickhill, Dunstable, St. Albans and Barnett—and the *Alliance* (from Liverpool) calls at the same Inn, every evening at 8; goes the same route as the mail.
To ATHERSTONE, the *Accommodation* (from Birmingham) calls at the Swan, every Monday, Thursday and Saturday evenings, at six.
To BIRMINGHAM, the *Accommodation* (from Atherstone) calls at the Swan, every Monday, Thursday and Saturday mornings, at nine.
To LIVERPOOL, the *Royal Mail* (from London) calls at the Swan, every morning at a quarter before eight (Monday excepted) through Lichfield, Rugeley, Stone, Newcastle, Congleton, Knutsford, Warrington & Prescot—and the *Alliance* (from London) calls at the same Inn, every morning at three; goes the same route as the mail.

CARRIERS.
To LONDON, all goods go by way of *Birmingham and Coventry.*
To ATHERSTONE, Joseph Smith, from his house, every Tuesday.
To BIRMINGHAM, Wm. Davey, from his house, every Monday, Thursday and Saturday—Jas. Nichols, from his house, every Thursday—Thomas Nurse, from the Green Man, every Tues—Jos. Smith, from his house, every Monday and Thursday—& John Whear's, &c., from his house, every Thursday.
To COVENTRY, Thomas Nichols, from his house, every Saturday—and Joseph Smith, from his house, every Friday.
To NUNEATON, Thomas Nurse, from Birmingham, calls at the Green Man, every Thursday.
To TAMWORTH, Joseph Smith, from his house, every Saturday.

List of trades in Coleshill taken from Pigot's Directory 1828/29

Chapter 9

AGRICULTURE

In many historical sources, Coleshill is referred to as a market town with a fine medieval church. Its importance increased during the 18th century partly because it was situated on the Great North Road. Many reasons have been put forward for Coleshill's prosperity then, including the direct influence of the Digby family who came to Coleshill in 1495 replacing the previous Lord of the Manor. Prior to this their lands were mainly in the East Midlands. The family moved to Coleshill and built a manor house, beginning a long association with the area. However the economic benefits of land enclosure and the national trends towards increasing agricultural efficiency may also have played a considerable part towards Coleshill's prosperity.

Coleshill was the centre of the Hemlingford Hundred and the whole parish was approximately 6,000 acres. To the south west of the parish was the Welsh Drove Road, now the Chester Road from Birmingham to Stonebridge, which ran from the hill pastures of Wales to the fattening pastures of the Midlands and then on to the great markets of London and the south. All the local roads converged on Coleshill as it was a market centre, as well as the main route from London to Holyhead in the 18th century.

It was a significant Warwickshire market town built on agriculture and communications. According to early records it had a thriving market selling livestock, dairy produce, grains, honey, wax, timber, charcoal, faggots, rabbits and other game. The soil consisted of Arden sandstone with a capping of glacial sands and gravels; below the glacial debris area was keuper marl. Coleshill was well watered by the rivers Blythe and Cole which joined the river Tame north of the parish boundary.

MEDIEVAL FIELD SYSTEMS AND CHANGES IN LAND USE

Coleshill's open field system is first recorded in 13th century deeds, but it was probably established earlier. These open fields were large tracts of arable land divided up into strips of about a third of an acre called selions, which were held by inhabitants of the manor.

Within the fields there were many internal divisions. Pasture for stock became scarce as meadowland was ploughed up into large open fields. Added to this was a whole mass of land, which lay in enclosed, hedged fields that had emerged out of the clearance or assarting of the woodlands in the 12th and 13th centuries. Much of the land that lay beside streams and the Blythe, Cole and Tame was used as meadow land to supply hay for winter feed. Animals grazed on Coleshill Heath, a large tract of heath land to the south of the parish, or in enclosed fields and closes which lay outside the open fields. The main medieval field crops grown throughout the Warwickshire Arden were wheat, barley, oats, peas and beans, and

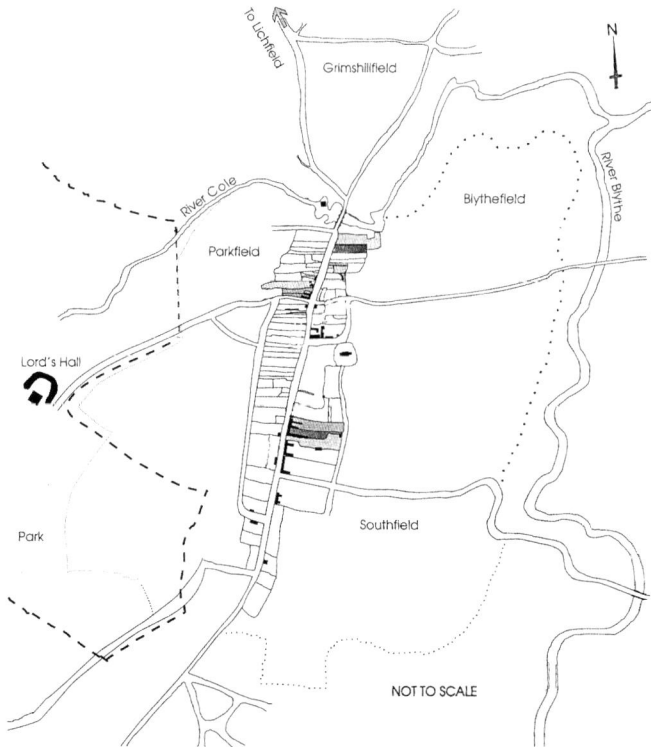

Coleshill and the original four fields before Enclosure in 1779

dredge, a mix of oats and barley.

During the later middle ages, especially in the 15th century, there were many changes in agriculture mainly due to devastating epidemics, which wiped out huge numbers of people, possibly around half the existing population. of the area. As a result large areas of arable land fell out of cultivation and pastoral farming became more important instead. The area became important as it provided rich fattening pastures for beef cattle at this time. The landscape became more enclosed, with small hedged and ditched closes, with some areas of open fields.

During a journey from Coleshill to Meriden in the late 1530s, John Leland the topographer observed 'the grownd in Arden' is muche enclosyd, plentifull of gres, but no great plenty of corne'. People clearing the land, which they held as freeholders, were settling the Heath End of Coleshill. The popular belief that the pattern of land was a direct result of 18th century enclosure is a myth. The four great open town fields, Blythefield, Grimesfield, Parkfield and Southfield, remained, along with the meadowlands of the Blythe, Cole and Tame. There was also some woodland, most noticeably Chelmsley Wood.

THE DIGBYS

The Digbys, as lords of the manor of Coleshill, were by far the largest landholders with both their demesne lands under their direct control, and the lands farmed by their tenants. A rental compiled for William, Lord Digby in 1745 lists 120 tenants. However, the family did not have complete control as some people owned closes or selions in open fields. Tudor Digbys began gradually buying up other freeholders so as to increase their share of ownership within the parish, and gradually consolidate their demesne lands. They contested and claimed the manor of Kingshurst from the Mountford family; this was in the parish of Coleshill. Similarly the manor of Sheldon was acquired.

The remaining manors, which the Digbys acquired, were purchased over a period of time. The manor of Marston Culy, which was in the parish of Bickenhill, was bought and remained in the family until 1818. They bought Gilson manor in 1716 and finally the manor of Alcott at the southwest end of Chelmsley Wood in the early 19th century. This demonstrates how, over a period of time, the Digbys' position in the area became stronger as they accumulated a string of manors.

As Lords of Coleshill, Sheldon, Marston Green, Kingshurst, Alcott and Gilson, it is not surprising that they had considerable impact on the area. Records of the Court Leet held in Coleshill of 1728 and those of Sheldon in 1734 show the rules designed to ensure reasonable maintenance of the lands; any fines were paid to the Lord of the Manor. Henry Digby, who had been granted an earldom in 1790, acquired other properties, including Wheeley Moor Farm which was owned by the Barton family. This steady acquisition of land continued well into the 19th century.

The Digbys were not unusual in holding vast quantities of land and properties for the 19th century was the age of the great estate in Britain when agriculture was the single largest source of wealth. However the Digbys, like many of their aristocratic contemporaries, did not farm themselves. They retained a marginal amount of land for their own use, while the remaining acreage was managed and rented by tenant farmers.

During the 18th century many members of the landed gentry improved their lands by further cultivating wastes and commons, improving farm buildings, encouraging soil improvement and above all, consolidating their farms to make them more efficient so that they could raise the rents. Many small farms were absorbed when a farmer died, leaving his land to his widow and children. Often the land would be divided into smaller parcels, which were later sold, as they were not viable. Farms consolidated into larger units became more efficient, simpler to manage and more profitable to the landlord, the tenant and the country as a whole.

In Coleshill, as in many rural towns, this increasing wealth led to the renovation of existing buildings, new buildings and the general prosperity of the area and many of its fine 18th century houses reflect this trend. At the heart of the Digby estate was the old park, whose manor house had been built by Sir William Mountford. The house and park were close to the western parish boundary by the river Cole, away from the town on the road to Bacon's End. The parkland was used to bolster the manorial finances, grassland was rented out, timber was sold off and rights were granted for grazing and pannage (the right to pasture pigs in a forest.)

The Digbys' growth in wealth and social standing was reflected in their house and park. The house was modernised and the park enlarged after the family bought many of the small closes to the south of the town. At this time the reason for the changes was unclear. It could have been for hunting and pleasure or purely for agricultural advantage. In 1699 Lord Digby ordered the construction of a new formal driveway, lined by an avenue of trees, which ran from Coleshill Hall across the fields to just below Heath End and avoided the town. He had negotiated to buy the necessary land from various small freeholders and although most of the driveway has now reverted to a grassy track and is criss-crossed by motorways, the section furthest from the Hall is still a road today, Hall Walk.

The Digbys had lived in Coleshill since 1495, but between 1783 and 1843 the main branch of the family moved from Coleshill to their estate at Sherborne Castle, Dorset. The Reverend William Digby lived in Coleshill from 1765 until his death in 1788. After the family's departure in the mid-18th century, the hall became deserted and run down and as absent lords of the manor their influence waned slightly.

LORD TORRINGTON wrote in his diary: -
Sunday, June 28th, 1789.

"I was up early, from a bad bed, and to the appearance of a cold low'ring morning; knowing that the park and seat of the Digby family was adjoining the town, I took my walk that way; here is an old park in wretched plight, and some mutilated avenues; but all the timber is gone; at present nothing can be more forlorn, tho' there is a running stream, capable of magnificence. The mansion house is very large, of the old striped sort, and was the seat of hospitality in the time of old Lord Digby, who lived in the beginning of this century the friend of the famous, and ever revered Dr. Hough, Bishop of Worcester. Being alone, and the rain falling fast I hurry'd back to breakfast; after which we sat confined gloomy by the weather; only sallying forth before service time to view the church."

17th century documents describe the vicarage buildings, the glebe lands and the customary tithes due to Coleshill vicarage. Most of the church lands appear to have been enclosed lands or closes rather than selions in the open fields. The vicarage contained a whole range of farm buildings, not just for tithe tributes but also to serve as a working farm. With the enclosed parcels of Southfield and Blythefield forming the core of the arable and pasture lands of the glebe, the vicarage buildings were extremely useful.

The family acquired two more important additions to the estate at the end of the 17th century, the manors of Kingshurst plus a sizeable tract of land and a large inn at Bacon's End. This land surrounded the Chester Road (also called the Welsh Road) an increasingly

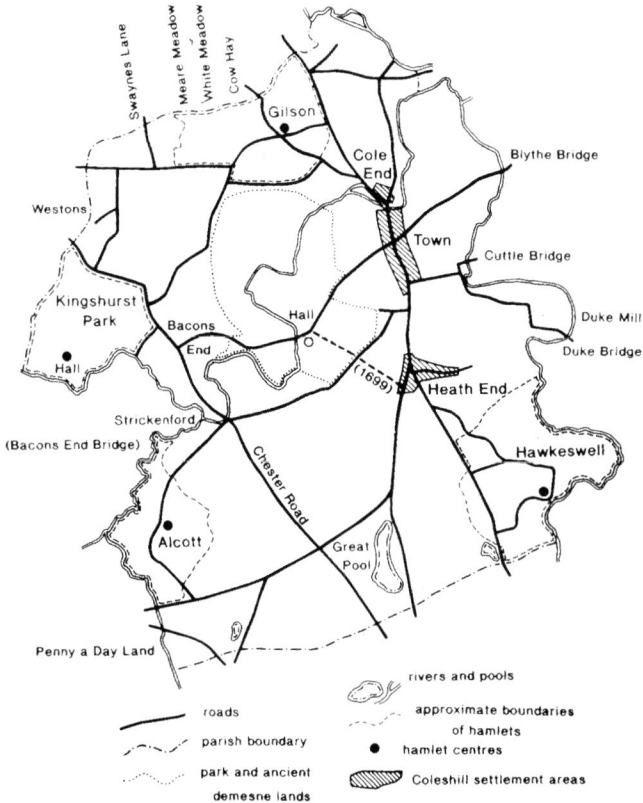

The principal topographical features of Tudor and Stuart Coleshill. (Drawn by Simon Hayfield)

important long distance route that passed to the south of Coleshill via Castle Bromwich and into Birmingham.

The land was rented back to the previous owner. Renting land at this time swelled Lord Digby's coffers substantially. While he was consolidating his demesne land in the district, records show that the erosion of the open fields in and around the parish of Coleshill was also growing. Oxen were no longer the principal beasts of burden. Horses had taken over as the main draught animals on Coleshill farms and fields and arable farming was still more prevalent than pastoral farming.

THE AGRARIAN REVOLUTION AND ENCLOSURE

The Agrarian Revolution of the 18th century had profound effects on the evolution of the English countryside. There was a growing use of machinery, selective breeding of livestock, the introduction of new crops, and improvements in cropping techniques. It is hard to find specific documentation of these in Coleshill, however a major factor in transforming the face of agriculture in the 18th century was enclosure, which finally broke up the older, communal system of farming which had existed for centuries. The open field system was beginning to fail, there was no freedom of choice in the type of crops to be grown and bad breeding habits were weakening the animal stock.

By the early 18th century many years of piecemeal enclosing had reduced the acreage of the open fields. To enclose land was to put a hedge or fence around a portion of open land and so prevent the exercise of common rights over it. The advantage of 'enclosure' was that the land or 'close' could be farmed in any way the owner chose. Across the country enclosure benefited the larger and more enterprising landowners by freeing them from the trouble of farming small tracts of land scattered around the parish. In Coleshill quite a few of these small parcels were farmed from homes in the town centre. Enclosure allowed these smallholdings to be consolidated into new larger fields, often as a single block with a new improved farmstead built in the middle, or with an original, substantial farmhouse extended by adding a new wing.

Examples of this remain in Coleshill today at Wheeley Moor Farm. Several farms had the names of the town fields or of the land enclosed eg. Southfields Farm, Park Fark, Springfields and Coleshill Heath Farm. Often the farmers held important offices within the town, reflecting their status and prosperity. The farms were often major employers of local labour as two thirds of the land was arable and therefore labour intensive.

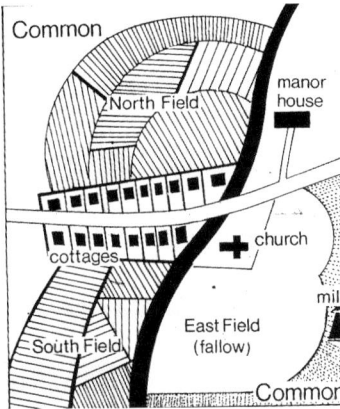

A village before enclosure

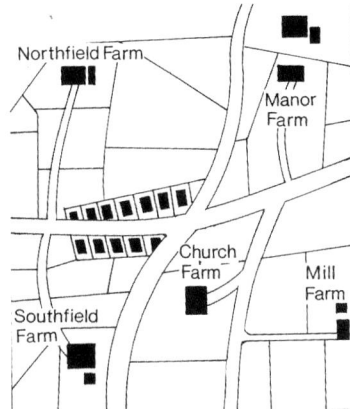

The same village after enclosure

Enclosure meant that the community lost its common grazing rights, however, occasionally the commons were over-grazed with too many animals. In theory an 'encloser' of land had to compensate the person for enclosure by surrendering some of his own common pasture rights. The loss of common grazing rights caused few problems when land was plentiful and enclosure took place without very much opposition. Many farms and indeed hamlets were created by the enclosure of waste land, which usually lay on the outer edges of parishes. It is likely that Heath End of Coleshill began like this and was recognised as a hamlet in the 18th century. The enclosure of the surviving common and open fields of Coleshill began in 1779 and took a year to formulate. The Enclosure Commissioners for Coleshill met at the Swan Inn, and formulated *'An act for dividing and inclosing the open and common fields and meadows, heath and*

104

wasteland and other commonable grounds in the parish of Coleshill'.
The only surviving map of Coleshill at this time is the 1783 estate
map by John Snape. This was completed three years after the
Enclosure Award and effectively serves as an Enclosure Map
showing the agreed division of Coleshill Heath and the remaining
open fields and common fields into new fields, new farms and in
some cases new roads.

The award says that the commissioners shall set out both public
and private roads through and over the new enclosures and
allotments stating the breadth of the roads. All turnpike roads and
also the road from Coleshill over Coleshill Heath towards Coventry
shall be and remain sixty feet broad between ditches. All other public
roads to be forty feet broad and between ditches except the bridle
paths and footpaths. All roads deemed to be necessary were named,
as were those that were going to be enclosed. Seven roads were
named, however one was to be kept as; ' a private path for the use of
the school lads'. The Commissioners would hear any complaints and
queries on a set day, the day to be published in Aris's Birmingham
Gazette and also a notice fixed to the church door. Any persons
objecting were desired to object in writing to the Commissioners.
Any roads no longer needed would be taken as part of the enclosed
land and then would be allotted. Henry, Lord Digby was going to
lose his rabbit warren when the heath was enclosed so he was going
to be compensated for the loss! Everyone who had grazing rights was
granted permission to continue to graze until the land was enclosed.

At this time Lord Digby owned the largest amount of land, but
his brother the Vicar of Coleshill, also had a substantial holding. The
High Street was still peppered with freehold interests that show that
Coleshill was far from being a 'closed' town, wholly owned by the
lord of the manor. The Enclosure award for Coleshill only involved
2,046 acres compared with the total parish size of 5,703 acres. It
largely dealt with the surviving remnants of the open fields and the
great swathe of hitherto unenclosed heath land on the southern
boundary of Coleshill.

Unlike many other villages, no map was drawn as an aid to
enclosure. Instead a vast manuscript 'Award' was prepared detailing
each new enclosure describing its boundaries, neighbours etc. The
large fields were divided by hedges and ditches into smaller fields of

varying sizes, ranging between two and 30 acres. The familiar pattern of blackthorn and hawthorn hedges was established and some have survived to the present day. Although farming became far more efficient, the social consequences were debatable. The poor were sometimes grossly injured by enclosure, even when they were compensated for their loss of common rights. The small piece of land they received was often worth far less to them than the right to graze, to get timber and bracken for bedding, and stones on the common. Enclosure helped to shape the landscape which we see around Coleshill today. The fields became smaller with hedges and ditches and often they were pastoral and not arable. New technology affected everyone's way of life and smallholders and cottagers suffered most through enclosure; cottage industries were no longer viable; they lost not just the right to graze their animals on the heaths and commons but often their cottage when the land was enclosed.

Unemployment increased and there was a housing shortage. The outbreak of the French war in 1793 created scarcities and prices rose sharply, wheat most of all, doubling by the end of the war. The farmers were able to maximise output, but little of their profit was passed on to the farm labourer. The population was also increasing. Enclosure certainly made farming more efficient and profitable and the whole parish appeared increasingly prosperous. Towards the end of the 18th century tenants farmed much of the Digby land and were the greatest beneficiaries of the new system.

CONTEMPORARY REFERENCES TO AGRICULTURE

Many publications of the time dealt with the subject of agriculture. Peter Lavery writing in 'Warwickshire of 1790' said that Coleshill was one of the towns privileged to hold a market to buy and sell produce, alongside Coventry, Birmingham, Warwick, Stratford, Henley, Atherstone, Alcester, Kineton, Nuneaton, Rugby, Southam, Sutton Coldfield, Kenilworth and Bidford. He also noted that Coleshill had a weekly market and three annual fairs. Several books were published on the observations of Mr. John Wedge of Packington. He surveyed the County of Warwickshire and gave his opinions on the ways to improve agriculture and, particularly interestingly, on enclosure. In 1794 he describes how many of the enclosed fields are now converted from arable to pasture land, grazed by improved breeds of cattle and sheep, and need far fewer hands to manage them. He observes that the farms have generally become much larger and writes, "*the hardy yeomanry of country villages have been driven for employment into Birmingham, Coventry and other manufacturing towns, whose flourishing trade has sometimes found them employment.*" He notes that if trade and manufacture should drop, the real consequences of enclosure would be seen.

Many of the poor now worked in manufacturing towns and thousands of farm workers were also employed on canal building. Wedge comments on the large population increase in the county, (this was true of Coleshill at the end of the century) and declares that we should think ourselves very fortunate to be so close to Coventry and Birmingham. The urban workforce earned about 25% more than country folk, even at harvest time.

Wedge observes that the rivers and streams in the county have been very much neglected, becoming narrow, full of plants and rushes and often flooded. The exception was the River Blythe which the Earl of Aylesford had cleared, using the soil as manure and preventing many summer floods. Wedge also comments that Aylesford had a large flock of excellent Wiltshire sheep and fine cows, as a direct result of his much improved pastures. Boggy and waste areas were drained in 1780 and Wedge remarks that although Coleshill and Bickenhill heaths are still of an inferior quality, some parts of them will soon become useful land.

In 1813 Coleshill is still ranked as an important market town by Adam Murray, a land-surveyor and estate agent who praises enclosure within the County of Warwick and claims that the benefits are felt throughout the county. He writes

"*The land that formerly supported half starved sheep, is now yielding abundance of both grass and corn.*" He also recommends that farmers do not grow corn because the cheap imports from Germany, Denmark and other Baltic ports will destroy their livelihood, and he points out that the grass farmer will have a better chance of survival.

Murray also comments on Lord Aylesford's purchase of Spanish or Merino sheep for their superior wool and greater weight than South Downs. In 1814 an account in 'Beaties of England and

Wales' declares that Coleshill is not considered a principal seat of Warwickshire, as the landowner is no longer a resident in the county. It describes the park to the west of the town, but records that the mansion is entirely taken down.

Pigot's Trade Directory of 1828 records that *"Coleshill is a small market town and parish, in the Birmingham division of the ward of Hemlingford, 103 miles from London, 18 miles from Warwick and about 9 miles from Birminham and Atherstone; pleasantly situated on a hill of considerable height, watered by the Cole. Over the river is a good stone bridge...Coleshill is well watered; besides the rivers Cole and blythe there are several fine pools, covering from 20 to 100 acres; the meadows are rich and the vacinity of the town is adorned with beautiful hanging woods...The market day is on a Wednesday, and the fairs are, the Monday before Shrove Tuesday, May 6th, and the Wednesday after Michaelmas day, chiefly for horses and all kinds of cattle".*

CHANGES IN THE GEORGIAN PERIOD

From the available records it appears that Coleshill evolved and developed throughout the 116 years of the Georgian period. The number of houses and the population steadily grew from 1714 until 1800, when this increase became most noticeable. Older houses were often given a 'new look' with stucco rendering or a stone facing to emulate the fashion of the day, however the overall pattern of the town hardly changed.

This is not true of agriculture. At the beginning of the Georgian Era, Coleshill still had large tracts of heath and common land as well as open arable town fields. Enclosure had been practised in a small way both by the landlord and also by people who had settled or squatted on the wastelands and heaths, building modest dwellings and enclosing the land.

HORSE RACING AND A GRINNING CONTEST

There is evidence that prior to the enclosures, Coleshill people enjoyed colourful leisure pursuits on the surrounding heath. In 1711, 70 years before the heath was enclosed, Addison, one of the authors of a famous series of essays for the Spectator magazine, described the bizarre goings-on with gusto and amazement. Addison used to stay at the Swan, and this essay, number 173 of the collection, bears the date 'Tuesday, Sept. 18, 1711'.

"On the 9th of October next will be run for upon Coleshill Heath in Warwickshire in Warwickshire, a Plate of 6Guineas, 3 Heats, by any Horse, Mare or Gelding that hath not won above the value of 5£, to carry 10 stone weight if 14 hands high, if above or under, to carry or be allowed weight for inches, and to be entered Friday the 5th at the Swan in Coleshill, before 6 in the evening. Also a Plate of less value to be run by Asses. The same day a Gold Ring to be Grinn'd for by Men.

"The first of these diversions, that is to be exhibited by the 10£ Race-Horse, may probably have its uses; but the two last, in which the Asses and Men are concerned, seen to me to be altogether extraordinary and unnacountable. Why they should keep running Asses at Coleshill, or how making Mouths turn to account in Warwickshire, more than in any other Parts of England, I cannot comprehend. I have looked all over the Olympick Games, and do not find anything in them like an Ass race, or a Match at Grinning. However it be, I am informed that several Asses are now kept in Body-Clothes, and Sweated every Morning upon the Haeth, and that all the Country Fellows within ten Miles of the Swan grinn an Hour or two in their Glasses every morning, in order to qualifie themselves for the 9th of October. The prize which is proposed to be grinn'd for has raised such an Ambition among the Common People of Out-grinning one another, that many very discerning Persons are afraid it should spoil most of the Faces in the County; and that a Warwickshire Man will be known by his Grinn, as Roman Cathholicks imagine a Kentish man by his Tail. The Gold Ring which is made the prize of Deformity, is just the Reverse of the Golden Apple that was formerly made the prize of Beauty, and should carry for its Poise the old motto inverted

    Detur tetriori.

Or to accomodate it to the Capacity of the combatants

    The frightfull'st Grinner

    Be the winner."

So did the enclosure of the heath, curtail any of these homely amusements? Certainly horse sales continued there for another century but with enclosure restricting the space available, so far there is no evidence that the horse-racing and grinning matches survived into Victorian times.

GROWING PROSPERITY

With the Enclosure Act of 1779 came a major upheaval. Lord Digby had benefited from enclosure as he now had a new and increased source of wealth. The farms he owned were now much larger and rented by tenant farmers, who increased both the landlord's prosperity and their own. They were able to farm much more productively by choosing the crops and animals suitable to the land. Farm machinery replaced some of the manpower previously needed and the labour they required could be hired and dismissed as and when required.

The increasingly prosperous farmers had a ready outlet for their produce at the country market at Coleshill, but more importantly the two cities of Coventry and Birmingham needed feeding. The produce could be moved around the country more efficiently by improved roads and canals. People were displaced from their homes and their common rights were removed. Even with compensation, hardship for the poor had increased; the cities offered employment, but how this affected the citizens of Coleshill is unknown so far.

Despite all the data available, it is not clear exactly why the population of Coleshill increased dramatically from 1800 and whether this was due to a wider range of occupations attracting the work force to stay or better health care coupled with more food. Whatever the reasons, the town prospered and its housing, farmhouses and outbuildings reflect this. Lord Digby and his family now lived at Sherborne Castle in Dorset. Tenants farmed most of his lands and he collected the rent, benefiting considerably from enclosure. During the earlier part of the Georgian Era the Digbys' influence was felt in the social prestige they had generated in the area, in education, the church, the law, the people and later the landscape, finance and property.

In the administration of the charities, land they had donated provided a good and reliable source of revenue. In the church there is ample evidence of their contribution, particularly that of the sixth Lord Digby's brother William, who was vicar of Coleshill between 1765 and 1788 and also Dean of Durham. The Coleshill that emerged after the turn of the century was more prosperous than it had been for the previous hundred years. The Digby family, as Lords of the Manor and the greatest landholders, certainly contributed enormously to what we understand as the agrarian revolution in Coleshill and its increased wealth

The Workhouse in Workhouse Lane (now Blythe Road) by Valerie Preece.

An artists representation of a punishment treadmill.

Royal Mail Coach on a flooded road by Pollard.

Market Hall and Pillory by David Rees from an old print.

The stocks and pillory on Church Hill, Coleshill. Photograph by Mavis Cave.

Georgian doorway at Springfield House.

Miss Joan Tuckley at her family's ironmongers shop, High Street, Coleshill. Civic Society 1985.

The Green Man public house.

St Andrew's House, Coleshill.

Chapter 10

COLESHILL'S GEORGIAN CHURCHES

COLESHILL PARISH CHURCH

The church of St Peter and St Paul whose fine tower and spire make it a landmark for miles around, stands at the top of Church Hill. Before its restoration in 1859, it was hemmed in by houses on the west and north-west and in Georgian times, it would have looked far more cluttered and without the spacious setting it enjoys today. However, the parishioners of that era would have benefited greatly from the improvements to the interior of their church, which began in late 1700:

Copy of an old print of Coleshill Parish Church

The Parish Records described how:
" This church lay long neglected, very squalid, and ruinous and without ceiling quite open to the tiles. The floor very uneven, laid, in some parts with square tiles (but of very unequall size) in some parts with bricks, and in all others rough stones. The seats were some

112

much higher than others; of different wood, viz; some were oak, some of Deal and others of Elme, not two of them together of like worke, or proportions; and almost all of them shamefully patch'd."

In 1700 the church wardens, Mr John Brookes and Mr Thomas Mason. *"Repaired the Roof of the Church, takeing away the decayed, and weak Timber thereof, and supplying it with new, sound and strong timber in all places."*

Much encouraged by this work: *"In April following, viz 1701 the Right Hono. William Lord Digby began to beautifie this house of God, arching or ceiling with Lath and Plaster (at his own proper charges) the Great, viz the Middle Isle thereof, adding the Ornamental Garnish."*

The inhabitants moved by this *"pious example and having the use of his lordship's scaffolds... Did presently agree to ciel the other two isles of the Church, viz in the North and South Sides; which Mr John Brookes and Mr Mason, church wardens, also for that year, viz 1701 did that same summer."*

Work continued, replacing the pulpit, with the stairs and a reading seat, plus seating for the master and scholars of the free school. The floor was levelled and the middle aisle was laid with square polished stones. The steeple was separated from the church with a *"decent screen of carved wood"*. Steps of Lewn stone were laid into the church from the north and south doors and uniform seating for the congregation was installed.

During this period, Mrs Elizabeth Martingall bequeathed a velvet pulpit cloth and cushion to the church. Her brother, Mr John Elsmere, disputed her bequest, but compromised by offering £10 which the church wardens accepted. They bought a blue velvet pulpit cloth and cushion with a gold and silken fringe, with the money, Lord Digby offering to pay the difference *"out of his own farther bounty"*.

By 1714, with the parish church *"beautified"* and more comfortable than it had ever been, the flow of gifts continued.

THE HISTORY OF THE FIRST WESLEYAN CHAPEL OF COLESHILL

In 1999 Coleshill Civic Society acquired a bundle of deeds and deposited them in their archives. On studying the bundle, it was found to relate to land at Church Hill in Coleshill, just below the old grammar school. A messuage or tenement on this land later became a Wesleyan Chapel or meeting-house.

According to the abstract of title, Henry Smith of Coventry sold land to Michael Wade of Whoberley, Warwickshire in 1626, described as *"all that close or pasture known as Nun Orchard"*, then occupied by Edmunde Oulder, beside a highway leading from Coleshill churchyard to a common field called Blyth Field.

In 1702 Thomas Mason of Coleshill, malster, bought this land and *"the newly erected tenement situate in Coleshill near the School House, built upon Nun Orchard"*. The Masons owned the land for the next 120 years, Thomas Mason passing it on to Gustavo Mason in 1723 with Thomas Mason inheriting in 1760. On his death in 1806, his daughter Sarah inherited it.

From 1806 to 1809 the property changed hands several times. Sarah appears to have sold it to John Dale of Coleshill who sold it to Thomas Rathbone, who mortgaged it to Thomas Arme. By this time it was described as being *"two tenements, garden, barkside (or backside) pump and well, next to the Free School of Coleshill"* and *"adjoining a close by the name of Nun Orchard"*, with a large *"barn and fold"* nearby.

However, after these three years the property now described as *"two messuages or tenements with brewhouse"* once more came into the hands of the Masons, when it was sold in 1809 by Thomas Rathbone to a John Mason, Coleshill's first Methodist. In 1810, Mason obtained a certificate from the Bishop of Lichfield (discovered in the bundle of deeds) granting him the right to use *"a house situate in Church Hill in the Town of Coleshill in the County of Warwick... as a place of Public Worship for the use of Protestant Dissenters according to an Act in the first year of King William and Queen Mary exempting their Majesties' Protestant Subjects, dissenting from the Church of England, from the penalties of certain laws"*.

114

By 1826 the chapel and its membership were fully established, for John Mason sold the building to the Methodist Church for £264 and moved on to the Methodist Mission House, London. Twelve trustees were appointed:

James Heeley,	steel toy maker of Birmingham.
John Hope,	button maker of Birmingham.
John Colwell,	cord wainer of Birmingham.
William Brown,	cord wainer of Birmingham.
Samuel Hickling,	chemist of Birmingham.
Joseph Aston,	gun maker of Birmingham.
Thomas Aston,	rule maker of Birmingham.
William Swinburn,	butcher of Birmingham.
Thomas Hickling,	chemist of Aston.
John Allen,	gilt toy masker of Aston.
Richard Griffiths,	glass maker of Aston.
Charles Smallwood,	cooper of Coleshill.

According to the deeds, one of the trustees' duties was to ensure that the appointed preacher preached no other doctrines that those contained in John Wesley's 'Notes on the New Testament, 1784', and the first four volumes of the sermons. Further, if any preacher were immoral in his conduct, erroneous in doctrine, or deficient in his abilities as a preacher, then the trustees were required to call the other preachers of the district and the leaders of the circuit to come to their chapel and sit in judgement.

By 1854 the chapel must have become too small or otherwise inadequate, for the trustees sold it to the Earl of Digby, the hereditary Lord of the Manor of Coleshill for £460 with the consent of the Methodist Conference. For the first time since it was built, over a century before, a sketch map is provided showing that the chapel stood just below the old Grammar School, on a site now occupied by a detached house, 'Elinor', on Church Hill. The 17 trustees at the time of the sale are all listed, together with their signatures and seals.

It was presumably around this time that a new chapel was built in Wingfield Road, opposite the old 'Back Lane' School, as it was photographed before the present Methodist Church in Coventry Road was built in 1900.

It has been fascinating to record the early years of Methodism in Coleshill, only uncovered by the finding of a bundle of old deeds.

ST. LEONARD'S CHURCH, OVER WHITACRE

The first mention of a church at Over Whitacre was in 1203 when the Lord of the Manor, Jordan de Whitacre, sold the advowson, (the right of presentation), of Whitacre for twenty shillings to the Prioress of Markyate in Bedfordshire.

St Leonard's, Over Whitacre in Georgian times

The present church of St. Leonard's was built in 1765 by either William or David Hiorn. They were mason architects of the mid 18th century, and were also responsible for work on Farnborough Hall, Stoneleigh Abbey and the Shire Hall in Northgate Street, Warwick. St. Leonard's consists of a chancel, nave and west tower with a spire,

116

all built in local red sandstone. The present exterior is little altered from Hiorn's building apart from the spire, which was erected in 1850 and replaced the dome or cupola, which had been built in 1765.

A set of communion plate, a flagon, paten and cup given to Over Whitacre Parish by Lord Digby in 1734

The interior of St. Leonard's consists of a shallow chancel and nave with a west gallery. There is a small porch inside the base of the tower and above this is a choir vestry-cum-bell chamber. Two bells hang in the western tower. The smaller strikes E flat and is thought to date from the 14th century, while the larger strikes A sharp and was cast at Leicester in 1616.

Chapter 11.

GEORGIAN SCHOOLS

COLESHILL GRAMMAR SCHOOL

By the Georgian period, Coleshill Grammar School had been in existence for several centuries, probably since the late middle ages when it was founded as a chantry school, one of many set up at that time. A chantry was a foundation where daily or weekly services, usually masses, were celebrated for the souls or good estate of various people. They usually involved a priest performing specific liturgical duties, such as praying for the souls of the founder and their relations.

The scale of such chantries varied enormously. Some were newly built chapels with more than one priest; others were more modest affairs, established within an existing church, with either a chantry priest or a member of the parish clergy supplementing his income by conducting the chantry services. Often the founder specified that the chantry priest should teach children to help him celebrate the mass by saying or singing certain passages from the service. A chantry existed in Coleshill church before the end of the middle ages.

The Mountford family, who were lords of Coleshill between 1354 and 1495, considered creating a chantry at various times during the 15th century, but the best evidence of such a foundation comes from the beginning of the 16th century, via the will of Alice Digby, widow of Sir Simon Digby, who had died in 1519. Following the attainder or forefeit of Simon Mountford's lands on grounds of treason, the Digbys had been granted the manor of Coleshill in 1495, for their loyalty to Henry VII, and they still hold it. In her will of November 30th, 1520, Alice made provision for a modest chantry service in Coleshill church, leaving land to supply rents to pay a priest to celebrate daily masses for the souls of herself and her family as well as *"all Cristen soules"*.

The priest was also to train children to assist him with certain parts of the service, such as singing the Paternoster (Lord's Prayer), Ave (Hail Mary), and Credo (Creed). This opportunity was to be available to every child of the town under the age of 9, providing that their parents were householders. Interestingly it was open to both boys and girls as the will said *"by hytt a man childe or a woman childe"* and the youngsters were rewarded for their attendance with one silver penny on each occasion.

Alice Digby's will was the biggest single contribution towards a chantry in Coleshill church, but other parishioners made several more modest bequests at about the same time. When combined they provided a good income for a chantry service.

In 1507 Richard Chapman of Coventry, but clearly a native of Coleshill, left all his lands and tenements in Coleshill to provide a rent of 4s 4d to finance an almshouse for poor people at a place called "Chapman's" in Coleshill, 2s to pay for candles to burn before the cross in the church, and 1s to pay for obits, or annual masses to commemorate the dead, for his relations. John Green, vicar of Wombourne, near Wolverhampton, was also probably originally from Coleshill and in 1511 he left the rents from his messuage and lands in Coleshill to support a chantry service in the parish church. Similarly in 1519, Edmund Toppe, a well-to-do member of the community, who had been constable of Coleshill the previous year, bequeathed land to pay for an obit after Lady Day, and to pay for masses for the souls of his parents and immediate family. In 1522 Henry Everton, a yeoman from Heath End, the cluster of dwellings at the edge of the commons around Pound Lane to the south of Coleshill, left 2s 4d to pay for a priest to celebrate mass at the altar of the Virgin Mary. By the mid 1520s Coleshill church had therefore received a number of pious bequests of land and money for chantry uses, probably at the altar to the Blessed Virgin Mary in the south aisle of Coleshill church.

Although the school was probably founded in 1520 it was not recorded until 1563, the year in which Simon Bellars granted two annuities to the *"guardians of the school"*. This reveals that by the reign of Queen Elizabeth the school was well established and its day-to-day administration overseen by 12 trustees. An early 17th-century memorandum lists gifts of property being made to the school in the 1550s, while occasionally some townsmen made small bequests in their wills towards the school, such as Henry Smith, a tailor, who died in 1573 and left *"a noble to the free schole."*

119

As with many other schools in the area, the teaching took place in the adjacent Church House, a kind of medieval parish room, where the social functions of the parish where held. A clue to this is given in the Commissioners report of 1613, which describes a messuage, cottage, or tenement *"in or near the churchyard site"* where a free school had previously been kept. This undoubtedly occupied the same site on Church Hill beside the church where the old Grammar School building still stands. Tudor grammar schools were usually small, often with only one teacher and 20 to 30 boys in one room. The school day was up to 10 hours long and mostly spent reading, writing, and speaking Latin.

The school appears to have lapsed by the early 17th century. In 1613 Commissioners appointed under the Statute of Charitable Uses by James I's government came to Coleshill to enquire into the school and other charity lands in the parish. After hearing evidence at the Swan, they reported that the school had been very generously endowed, receiving rents from 8 properties, 7 of which were in Coleshill and one in Coventry, as well as the monies from meadow lands and strips in the open fields of the parish.

By an article of agreement on July 17th 1613, Lady Abigail Digby and 7 other inhabitants of Coleshill, were trying to buy out other people who had acquired an interest in the school lands. They were going to use part of the money to repair the school building, while £60 was to be used to compensate Sarah Cowper, who was by then holding some of the school lands. In 1614 the Trustees appointed a new schoolmaster and an usher, roles which probably corresponded to the later posts of headmaster and second master respectively.

Second masters were styled ushers well into the 19th century. Little is known of the school in the 17th and 18th centuries. In 1700 it was recorded that Coleshill Grammar School Library housed over 400 volumes, mainly about theology. A new master, George Burgess, was appointed as usher to start teaching up to 20 poor boys writing and accounts at Michaelmas 1769, with an annual salary of £5.

After his death he was replaced by a Mr Taylor, who was to be paid annually £20 to teach all the boys of the parish who were *"fit to be admitted"*, 20 poor boys, and any from outside the parish who paid. Mr Taylor was to have *"free use of the school, writing desk, seats and benches, except the seats for the Latin scholars at the upper end of the school, reaching from the Latin master's desk to the fireplace, which must be reserved for the sole use of the Latin master and his scholars."*

The Grammar School, Church Hill

An inventory made of the building in October 1794 gives a good indication of the school towards the end of the 18th century. Apart from the schoolroom, this lists all the rooms of the school and describes their contents. On the ground floor was a well equipped kitchen, a parlour, and the best parlour. On the first floor was a chamber over the best chamber, a chamber over the schoolroom, a chamber over the kitchen, and what was probably the headmaster's bedroom. This was called the Chamber over the Little Parlour, and it contained a bedstead, a hanging and window curtains, two

121

featherbeds, two bolsters, a pillow, a dressing table and chair, a closestool, or commode, with pan.

On the second floor were four small rooms or garrets, which contained sparse furnishings and bedding, and were probably occupied by the few boys who boarded. One of these, the *"Garrat on the right hand"* also housed some ironmongery and kitchenware, and the scholars may have prepared and eaten their meals mainly in this room. There was also a brewhouse, with a copper, a *"brass boyler"*, and a bottle rack, as well as a cellar.

Thomas Line, who compiled the inventory, recorded at the end that *"the pewter dishes and plates are in their present state totally unfit for service"* and added that in the chamber over the kitchen and in the little parlour, the *"curtains of the beds are so decayed by time that it is necessary to replace them with new ones"*. When another headmaster, Mr Rathbone, joined the school in 1798, the trustees agreed to build a brewhouse and a coalhouse for him. Following the death of the Reverend John Davie in June 1822, a new headmaster, the Reverend George Salmon, was appointed at an annual salary of £80, and required by the trustees to teach and instruct all the boys of the parish. The school house was described as being *"a late, substantial building adjoining the Churchyard.and comprise a large room occupied hitherto by all scholars of the parish, the children of Paupers as well as Classick Pupils, and from, a deficiency of Room it is thought necessary and requisite to separate the Latin scholars from the English and for which progress the Trustees will erect a new building adjoining to the present one as a second school room for the Classical School"*.

The Trustees allocated £600 to pay for this, but Salmon was apparently so appalled by the condition of the school, that he offered to donate £100 from his own salary to build two new schoolrooms. In 1824 it was reported that the schoolmaster's house was in such a poor state that it was demolished and a new house with two adjoining schoolrooms was constructed at a cost of £1000. Within the new building were upper and lower rooms for teaching. It was reported that boys were admitted to the Lower School as soon as they could read the New Testament, and they were taught English and Writing, Accounts and Geography. This part of the school was taught by an under master, who received £70 a year.

He had no residence, but was expected to pay for his own assistant from his salary. By the 1820s more than 50 boys were educated in this room. In the Upper School, or Classical School, a boarder and some 5 scholars were instructed in classics by the Reverend Salmon. Numbers had clearly declined by the 1830s as it was reported that within memory there had been 8 or 9 boarders, each paying fees of £100 a year, and eight day boys. Salmon resigned as Headmaster in 1837.

Chapter 12.

LAW AND ORDER

INTRODUCTION

One of the legacies of Magna Carta was the English attachment to trial by jury. *"No free man shall be imprisoned except by the lawful judgement of his peers."*

The English common law and its procedures were exported to British colonies across the globe, becoming a lasting legacy of Empire. Many early crimes were punished by whipping, branding and the stocks, with the death penalty reserved for so-called serious offences. The ultimate deterrent became common in the 18th century, as hunting became the preserve of the wealthy and fear of the poor troubled Parliament.

In many cases, some element of mercy allowed for transportation instead. Convicts, some still children, were shipped across the wild oceans to the Americas or the new lands of Australia to work as little better than slaves for the term of their sentence. Most did not return. The death of others provided mass-entertainment, and hanging days drew huge crowds. These 'holidays' stopped in 1868, when executions were moved inside prisons. Today the death penalty remains but only for treason and piracy.

CRIME & PUNISHMENT IN THE GEORGIAN ERA

Throughout the 18th and 19th centuries theft of various·sorts was the principal criminal offence. It was only towards the end of the Georgian era, in 1826, that the Home Secretary Robert Peel announced that he would begin his proposed consolidation and rationalisation of the Criminal Law.

He began with the laws relating to felony. Theft far exceeded the committals and convictions for any other type of offence and in 1825, 14,437 people were charged with various crimes, 12,500 for theft.

Crime in the early 18th century was rife in Britain. Footpads robbed people in the streets and highwaymen infested the roads.

Mercers (shopkeepers) lost goods to petty thieves and poachers robbed landowners of game. Rural criminals stole sheep, pigs, corn, hay, wood, turnips or poultry once or twice a year. Crime was perceived as a mainly urban problem with most thieves working in gangs as professional fraudsters.

The few prisons were mainly used to keep people awaiting trial and were not the places of punishment we know today. The 'Police system' depended on part-time constables and watchmen, mostly unpaid local men who volunteered or were chosen to serve for a limited period. They were generally men of some standing locally, often innkeepers or blacksmiths, who would pay someone else (either in beer or other goods) to do their shift for them, so the system was extremely corrupt.

The poor did not consider poaching a crime as game in its wild state was not deemed the property of any individual, hence the origin of the saying 'fair game'. Poaching was not restricted to the poor. Many 'gentlemen poachers' were prosecuted under the Game Laws for organising gangs of local men to poach game and fish for them!

Gleaning was considered an offence if the gleaner filled more than one apron with ears of corn, wheat or barley. Wood collecting was restricted to fallen branches; it was an offence to cut down green branches or living trees. However gathering wood for fuel, building, or even for a maypole, was seen as a customary right.

Woodworkers often claimed 'chips' shaved from wood when making articles like tables and chairs while tailors took 'cabbage' (pieces of cloth left over after cutting out). However in both trades larger pieces of wood or material were also often 'liberated'.

Hatters and shoemakers would frequently substitute cheaper materials for those supplied by their customers, then make up the order in the cheaper materials and sell the better quality merchandise, pocketing the money. All these offences, if discovered, were dealt with at the Summary Sessions and legislation was passed during the 17th and 18th centuries relating specifically to the theft of wood.

Examples of punishment from the Court of Common Pleas

1785   A case of theft was brought for gleaning.

1788   A judge declared that there was no specific right in common law permitting anyone to glean without the authority of the farmer who owned the land. Landowners did not use the 1788 judgement as an opportunity for a blanket assault on gleaning. It seems that the gleaners' case was supported by humanitarian and scriptural arguments. While gleaning continued to be justified in terms of customary rights, the taking of other produce such as turnips and vegetables from the land was not. Labourers still continued to consider it a perk.

1798   Five men were sentenced to seven years transportation for taking wood.

SUMMARY SESSIONS

These courts were held by a magistrate, often in his own parlour or the local tavern.

QUARTER SESSIONS AND ASSIZES

These were the higher courts where two magistrates dealt with more serious offences. Bail was rarely granted which meant a stay in jail for many months before coming to trial. There were only four quarter sessions and two assizes each year, a magistrate and 'petty jury' dealing with quarter sessions, while a judge and jury dealt with assizes.

PUNISHMENTS

Despite the wretchedness of poverty in Georgian times, even minor crimes were brutally punished. The stocks were used for petty local offences, the pillory for more serious public crimes like fraud or cheating. While awaiting trial, prisoners were usually given useless work to do. At Brixton Prison there was a treadmill, and it was estimated that some prisoners climbed the equivalent of 2,500 metres per day!

The worst punishments, execution or transportation to America, were used only for the most serious offences. Transportation was to Georgia, named in honour of George III, until the American War of Independence when alternative places had to be found and Britain's new colonies in Australia finally filled the gap.

126

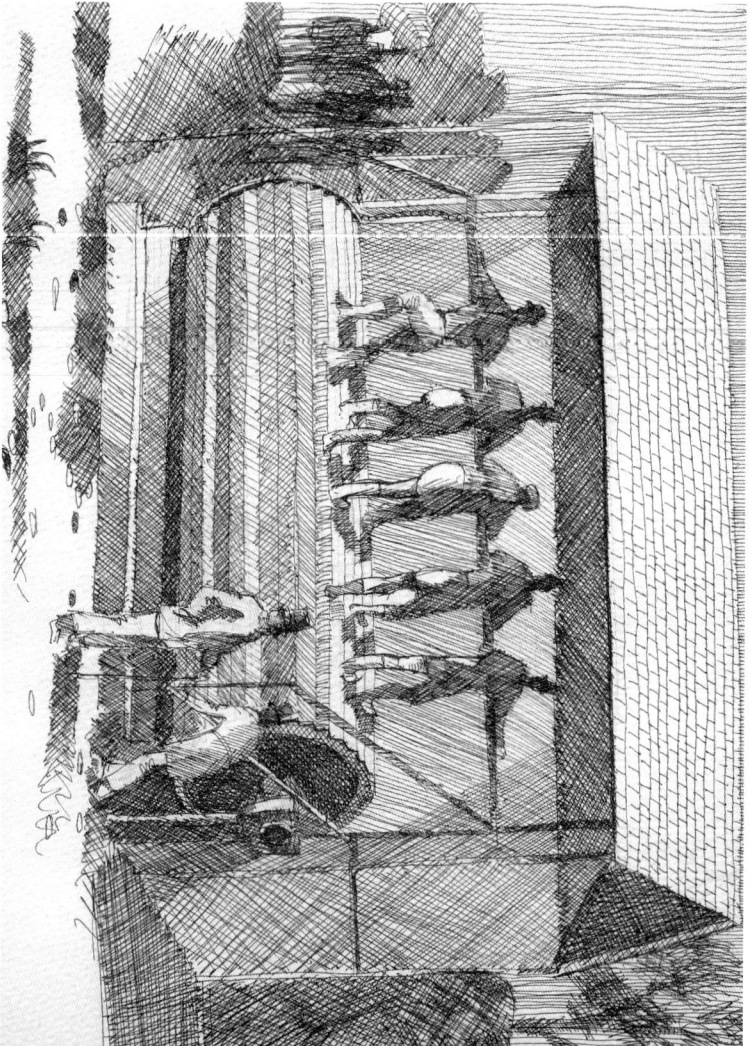

Punishment in Georgian Time: On the Treadmill.

THE STOCKS AND PILLORY

This ancient symbol of town justice originally stood in front of the old Market Hall in Church Hill, facing the High Street. The age of the stocks is uncertain but they are thought to be at least 17th Century in origin if not earlier. Few stocks of this type survive and these combined the functions of pillory, stocks and whipping post. The post is 14ft high supporting a platform standing board and a transom with holes for the head and hands. Lower down the post are the shackles for whipping, above a pair of shackles for the stocks. The contraption is last reported to have been used in 1863 when two Coleshill labourers were pilloried for drunkenness. In 1865 the old Market Hall was demolished and the stocks, which have recently been restored, were moved to their present position at the foot of Church Hill.

HIGHWAYMEN

The English highwayman is inextricably linked with myth and legend, in defiance of the mundane reality of his existence, a world away from the romantic fictions of daring, moonlit stagecoach hold ups by a masked hero on a jet black steed. Highwaymen worked alone, or in pairs or as part of a gang. Most were unheroic villains whose favourite targets were lone travellers. Only occasionally did they attack coaches. Most, like Dick Turpin, probably mixed robbery with other crimes such as burglary, poaching, smuggling and horse stealing.

A successful highwayman combined a steady nerve with the ability to shoot straight and ride well. The most famous were the sons of gentlemen, often forced onto the 'High Toby' by debt. Some were ex-soldiers unable to find work after returning from the wars and attracted to the life for the easy money it offered. Others were simply common cut-throats.

Every highway had its robbery black spots. In the Midlands, the main road from Birmingham to Warwick was among the most dangerous, while the Birmingham to Coventry route and the Chester Road around Sutton Coldfield also had bad reputations.

DICK TURPIN AND TOM KING

Dick Turpin, the most famous highwayman of all, was born John Palmer in 1705. He turned to highway robbery in partnership with Tom King a Birmingham highwayman from Sutton Coldfield. According to legend, the pair stayed at the Red Lion at Coleshill Road, Curdworth (now a private house). Tom King is said to have been caught and burnt to death in Sutton Park for his crimes and according to local legend, his ghost still haunts the spot. Dick Turpin was finally hanged at York in 1739 for stealing a horse.

Extract from the Coventry Mercury 29 December 1760: -

"On Wednesday morning last, about 5 o'clock the Warrington and Chester Stagecoaches were stopped on Meriden Heath by a single highwayman mounted on a brown or bay horse, who robbed the passengers in the Warrington Stage of about 4 guineas and those in the Chester stage of near 2 guineas. The villain lay on Monday and Tuesday nights last at the Bull's Head Inn, Meriden from which place he departed but a short time before he committed the above robberies, having ordered the hosteller to call him up by 4 o'clock in the morning. He is a middle sized man, wears a light coloured greatcoat and. was seen on Saturday last near Coleshill".

Although the number of highwaymen decreased, they were still operating in the late 1770's, but by the end of the 18th century, coaches were usually too fast and well guarded to be attacked. Roads were also improving and were therefore busier. It was the arrival of the Royal Mail coaches in 1784 which finally finished them off.

MAJOR LAWS PASSED IN THE GEORGIAN ERA

1723 Knatchbull's General Workhouse Act
1724 Single parishes were empowered to erect workhouses. Small parishes could form a union with others to make such a building viable. By 1776 there were about 2,000 workhouses in England.
1728 In Coleshill, a fine of 30 shillings was imposed on anyone carrying a naked flame along the streets (timber houses would probably still have been thatched).
1750 Local Acts

From this date, many areas promoted their own Acts of Parliament to obtain the power to levy a rate to pay for lighting and watching the streets.

1757 Militia Bill
Fear of a French invasion led to the Militia Bill, which in essence was the basis of today's modern Army. It then had a quota of about 32,000 men.

1800 Income tax was first levied to help pay for the war against France. In 1802, it was abolished, then revived in 1803.

1807 Local Militia Act
This allowed the raising of battalions of local militia in the counties. They were not liable to serve outside their own or adjacent counties. They were disbanded in 1816.

1816 Game Law Act
This limited the right to game to landowners only. The punishment for transgressions was transportation.

1816 The public Whipping of Women Law   *A Militiaman*
was abolished, but for men it continued until mid 1830's.

1817 Duelling was prohibited and treated as a criminal offence.

PUNISHMENTS

Larceny: Grand Larceny where goods stolen from a house were worth more than 12 pence, was a capital offence.

Petty Larceny of goods worth less than 12 pence brought a sentence of whipping. This was superseded in 1717 by transportation.

Stocks: A short spell in the stocks was a punishment known since Saxon times when each town and village had to provide stocks. The punishment had lapsed by the 1830's.

Whipping: This was a punishment particularly imposed on women and most parishes had whipping posts. Offenders were also whipped at the tail of a cart while it travelled along the main street. As late as 1740 prostitutes were whipped through the streets of London.

130

The Old Jailhouse Door (The Old Workhouse), 13 Blythe Road.

EXAMPLES OF CRIMES AND THEIR PUNISHMENTS 1714 to 1830:

DEATH SENTENCES

William Cooksey: for stealing seven heifers.

John Wade: for killing an ewe and taking away part of the carcase.

Sarah Bartlam: for stealing a silver watch.

Richard Cox: for stealing a horse.

John Buck & John Perry: for stealing a Calico bed-gown and three silk handkerchiefs.

TRANSPORTATION

Ann Anstey: seven years for pickpocketing 36s 6d (£ 1: 82p).

Rachel Tonks: 14 years for knowingly receiving a stolen silver watch.

George Morris: seven years for stealing a loaf of bread, a piece of bacon and 2lb of cheese.

PRISON TERMS / OTHER PUNISHMENTS

William Benner: Imprisoned for 12 months and fined 6d for stealing two flitches (sides) of Pork.

Jane Tate: 6 months in prison and a private whipping for stealing three pieces of black lace from a local Mercer.

Richard Dawson: sentenced to a public whipping for stealing some meat. The sentence was carried out at the Town's Friday market.

THE POLICE FORCE

When the police force was formed by Sir Robert Peel in 1829, their uniforms were blue, as this was a non-military colour and distinguished them from the Army, which had previously been used to enforce the law

THE COURT LEET

In 1728, the Digby family in Coleshill was granted a Court Leet, giving them the right to undertake duties of the Sheriff and appoint the petty constable for Coleshill.

This court eventually gained powers to try certain small criminal offences and the leet document reveals the detailed system of laws and punishments governing the lives of the people of Coleshill.

THE COURT LEET OF 1728

. P. Manorial Court of William, Lord Digby - 1728

Wee the Jurors att the Court Leet and Court Baron of the Right Honble the Lord Digby held for his Mannor of Coleshill in the County of Warwick at the Courthouse there on Fryday the five and Twentyeth Day of October 1728 beforw Edward Rocke gent. Steward there. Do make Ordain and Impose the severall pains and Bye Laws following (Viz.)

1.   Imp* Wee do order that all persons who have Mounds Trenches of ffences adjoyning to the Road leading from Pinfold Green to the farm grounds between the said Road and Cole Meadow or in the said Meadow shall sufficiently scour the same to them severally belonging so as to carry the water out of the said Road on or before the first day of December next or that every person making default shall forfeit to the Lord of this Manor for every neglect in the Name of a pain Twenty Shillings.

2.   And that every person who shall water hemp or flax in any of the Lord's Rivers or his Pools shall forfeit to the Lord of this Mannor for every such offence in the Name of a pain Ten Shillings.

3.   And that every person who hath any ffences or Mounds in or adjoyning to any the Cornfeilds or Lamas grounds or meadows within this Mannor shall sufficiently ffence the same to them severally belonging (Viz.) the Winter Corn feilds on or before St

133

Mathews Day And the Lamas grounds or Meadows on or before Candlemas Day next. And the Lent Cornfeilds on or before St Matthias Day next. Or that every person making a default shall forfeit for every offence to the Lord of this Manner in the Name of a pain Ten Shillings.

4.   And that every person who shall get sods or turfs on the heaths called Coleshill Heath and Bentsley Wood except within the bounds appoynted for that purpose or carry them so got of the said heaths or either of them, shall for every such offence forfeit to the Lord of this Mannor in the Name of a pain Ten Shillings.

And that every Certificated person who shall get turfe or sods or ling upon Coleshill Heath or Bentsley Wood shall forfeit to the Lord of this Mannor for every cartload of turfe, sods or ling so got in the Name of a pain Five Shillings.

6.   And that every person who shall get sods or ling upon Coleshill Heath or Bentsley Wood before St Georges day in any year shall forfeit to the Lord of this Mannor, for every load so got. In the Name of a pain Three Shillings and ffour pence.

7.   And that every person who shall leave or set Carts Waggons Plows or Harrows at all. Or shall suffer his or her Stalls to stand in the Streets except on Market Days and fair days or who shall leave or set any Tressles or Stalls under the Cross at any time. Or who shall set any horse or Mare under the Cross to hinder or obstruct the passage shall for evry or any of the offences aforesaid forfeit to the Lord of this Mannor in the Name of a pain Five Shillings.

8.   And that every person who shall stop the Water running from Cryers Well to Eaves Spring or Cole Meadow shall for every such offence forfeit to the Lord of this Mannor in the Name of a pain Five Shillings.

9.   And that every person who shall lay any Carrion or other Nusance or build houses of ease or hogstyes to the Annoyance of any

of their Neighbours shall for every such offence forfeit to the Lord of this Mannor in the Name of a pain Five Shillings.

10.   And that every person who shall put or tun any Hogs, Geese, Cattle or any sort of Poultry into the feilds before the Come be Inned shall be for every such offence forfeit to the Lord of this Mannor in the Name of a pain Five Shillings.

11.   And that every person who shall make any Inroachmint on the Lords Waste shall forfeit for every such offence to the Lord of this Mannor in The Name of a pain Five Shillings.

12.   And that every person within this Mannor who shall Harbour or Lodg any Vagrant or Travelling person above one night (Sunday only excepted) shall for every such offence forfeit to the Lord of this Mannor in the Name of a pain Ten Shillings. And to the person informing Three Shillings.

And that every person who shall suffer his, her or their Hogg or other swine to go upon any of the Comon or Waste ground within this Lordship.. .r.ing after one weeks notice to them given, shall for every such offence forfeit to the Lord of this Mannor in the Name of a pain Two Shillings and six pence.

14.   And that every person living within the Verge of the Ancient Town Well who shall neglect or refuse to pay his or her proportion or share towards the necessary repairs of the same shall forfeit to the Lord of this Mannor for such offence in the Name of a pain Five Shillings.

15.   And that every person keeping Market with Corn who shall open his or her Bagg or Baggs before the hour of Twelve in the aforenoon except three weeks befoer and three weeks after Mich; as shall be subject forever after to pay Tole to the Lord of this Mannor for all Corn by them brought into Market.

16.   And that every person who shall put or lay in the Streets any Dung. Ashes or any other matter to streighten or incumber the Way,

shall for every such offence forfeit to the Lord of this Mannor in the Name of a pain Five Shillings.

17.   And that every person who shall turn or suffer any Stabled horse or horses, mare or mares to go upon any the Common within this Lordship shall for every such offence forfeit to the Lord of this Mannor in the Name of a pain Ten Shillings.

18.   And that every person who shall carry fire in or along any Street within this Lordship otherwise than in a Lanthorn or Warming pan shall for every such offence forfeit to the Lord of this Mannor in the Name of a pain Thirty Shillings.

19.   And that every person who shall put on the Comon feild or Comon meadows or grounds within this Mannor above five sheep for a Day work, two cows for a Day work, one horse for a Day work or g…ing cattle proportionable shall forfeit to the Lord of this Mannor for every such offence in the Name of a pain Thlrty Shillings.

20.   And that every person who shall put or turn any sort of Cattle upon any the Comon fields, Meadows or Comon grounds within this Lordship and do not put his or her House Marke or two first letters of his or her name or some other known marke upon the same cattle shall for every such neglect forfeit to the Lord of this Mannor in the Name of a pain Twenty Shillings.

21.   And that every person who shall make Dams or Stanks in the Road to Damnifye their Neighbours shall for every such offence forfeit to the Lord of this Mannor in the Name of a pain Two Shillings.

22.   And that the Clerks of the Market for the time being shall on every Market Day between the hours of Eleavon and Twelve in the aforenoon come into the Market and weigh the Butter and all other matters weighable according to the Customs of the said Market and do all other things appertaining to their Office. And if they neglect or make default they shall for every such neglect severally forfeit to the Lord of this Mannor in the Name of a pain Ten Shillings.

23.   And that every person having land in Blythfeilds abutting on the Middle Highway leading to Cole Meadow Gate shall level their land ends to make the said way passable for waggons and Carraiges on or before the five and Twentyeth Day of December next or forfeit to the Lord of this Mannor any default or neglect in the Name of a pain Twelve Shillings.

24.   And that every Inhabitant of Hawkeswell shall well and sufficiently make or fence the mounds to them severally belonging round about the Winter Corn feilds there on or before the Fifth Day of November next or that every person Neglecting shall forfeit to the Lord of this Mannor in the Name of a pain Five Shillings.

25, And that Hugh Gardiner having the benefit of the Stalls near the Market place shall Cleanse the Way thro' the Cross for people to pass to Church on or before the Fifth day of November next. And so keep the same Weekly or forfeit to the Lord of this Mannor for every neglect in the Name of a pain Ten Shillings.

26.   And   we   do   Order   that   the   owners ………………………………………..trench   running   from   Cadd's piece by and through Gill Myre into ………. sufficiently scour the same to them severally belonging on or before St Andrews Day next. And that every person rnakeing default shall forfeit to the Lord in the Name of a pain Twenty Shillings.

27.   And that every person who shall Lay or Empty any Dung or other Nastiness into the Lane leading from the Town Well to Mt Shiptons shall forfeit to the Lord in the Name of a pain Ten Shillings.

28. And that the persons adjoining on both sides the same Lane shall Cleanse the same on or before the fourteenth Day of this Instant November on pain to forfeit to the Lord of this Mannor every person neglecting Ten Shillings (X)
Continued 1730
And that Thomas Falconridge Richard Brothers shall well and sufficiently scour their Ditches to them severally belonging between their own grounds and Southfeild on or before St Andrews Day on

pain that each person making Default shall forfeit to the Lord of this Mannor Five Shillings. (X)

29. And that Mr John Brooke and John Burton shall well and sufficiently make good the Path between Pinfold Green and Cole Meadow on or before Candle Mass day next on pain that each person neglecting shall forfeit to the Lord of this major Twenty Shillings. (X)

30. And that every person who shall happen not to sow his or her Winter corn before the first Day of November next shall not turn on any persons Lands or headlands being sowed with winter corn after that time but on their own lands. On pain that every person offending shall forfeit to the Lord of this Mannor Ten Shillings. (X)

Continued 1730
-And that every person who hath any Ditches between New Meadow and Haweswood feild and Down to the ford and between the Meadow and the feild shall scour the same and make the fences to them severally belonging on or before St Andrews Day next on pain that every person neglecting shall forfeit to the Lord of this Mannor Ten Shillings. (X)

-And that Thomas Smith and Samuel Bosworth shall scour their Ditches between Pitt Meadow and New Meadow on or before St Andrews Day next on pain that each person neglecting shall forfeit to the Lord of this Mannor Ten Shillings. (X)

-And that the ocoupyers of the Lands on each side of the Lanes called Pains Lane and Blythe Lane shall Cutt the Hedges to them severally belonging on or before St Andrews Day next on pain that each person neglecting shall forfeit to the Lord of this Mannor Five Shillings.

Witness our Hands: June Barton, Though Atkins, John Harris. John Hindley, Richard Harrison, William Walker. Saml. Cole, Th.Gree...gh. Robt. Dormer, George Wood, Sali. Smith. Win. Lowe. mc. Bruce. Tho. Shakespear

We the Jurors whose Names are Under Written at the Court Leet and Court Baron of the Right Honble the Lord Digby held the Eight and Twentyeth Day of October Anno Domini 1729 Do Order that all and every the first eight and Twenty pains and Bye Law and the last pain or Bye Law made the Last Court shall stand so and remain in as full force as if the same had been again partictularly Ordered by us.

-And we do Order that William Eaves. George Wood, Mr John Brooke and Wm Smith shall scour the trenches in Cole Meadow to them severally belonging and lay Planks or Bridge over the same so as to make the foot Way there passable on or before the Eleaventh Day of November next or that any person makeing default shall forfeit to the Lord of this Mannor Five Shillings.

-And we do Order that the Tennants or Occupyers of the Lands on bothe sides of the Lane leading from Shustoke toward Curdworth Bridge shall severally scour the Ditches to them severally belonging in good and sufficient manner on or before St Andrews Day next and that Samuell Hillman shall scour his trench down the Gosty ground so as to Draw the Water out of the said Road or Land on or before St Andrews Day next on pain that every person makeing default shall forfeit to the Lord of this Mannor for such his Neglect or Default in the Name of a pain Ten Shillings.

-And we d Order yt; ye Tenants or Owners of the Lands in Cole Meadow against Grimstock feild shall sufficiently repair the foot Way leading from Coleshill to the Forge Mill or keep the same repaired on or before St Andrews Day next. Or any persons makeing Default shall for each his Neglect shall forfeit to the Lord of this Mannor in the Name of a pain 10s.

-And we do Order that Widd Haycock shall scour her Ditch leading down to the River between her Land and Walter Colesleys on or before Christmas next or forfeit to the Lord of this Mannor in the Name of a pain 13s 4d

-And we do Order yt Ambrose Chetland, Widd. Overton, Humphery Lingard and John Smith shall sufficiently make the Fences to them severally belonging and continue the same so made between Hawkeswell Meadow and Millam Nook on or before Candlemass Day next Or that any person makeing Default shall for any such neglect or Default forfeit to the Lard of this Mannor in the Name of a pain Six Shillings and eight pence.

- And we do Order that the Widd Overton shall sufficiently scour her Ditch between her Orchard and Ambrose Chetlands land on or before Christmas Day next or forfeit to the Lord of this Mannor in the Name of a pain 6s 8d.

Witness our Hand
Joseph Cole. William Lowe, Geo Burgess. Will Gamel. Tho Eaves, Tho Smith, Thomas Drakefords, John Clifton, Will Mayow, John Overton, Humphreay Lingard, Robt Tysall.

(Entries culminating in an (X) had been crossed out later, for reasons now unknown.)

Chapter 13

GEORGIAN CHARITIES

Coleshill's Georgian charities are listed in the 14th report of the Commissioners, commonly known as Lord Brougham's Commission and compiled between 1819 and 1837. Most were linked closely with the parish church, St. Peter and St. Paul and only regular churchgoers could expect help in bad times. The vicars were exclusively members of the squire's family, so the landlord and the clergy held huge power over the lives of the poor.

The total gross income of charitable trusts is reported as £ 444 4s 2d .

A *"former income"* is listed as £ 297 16s 4d, so presumably the first figure referred to the income in 1837. It was mainly derived from property rent, dividends and interest.

The lion's share of charitable bequests was devoted to education, mainly through the Grammar School Trust, which had grown out of the Alice Digby Charity, established in 1520, to pay children for saying Paternosters, Aves and Credos for Alice, her husband, Simon Digby and their children.

In 1708 Lord Digby endowed and furnished a house to establish *"a school for the education of poor girls in Christian knowledge, and in other things and works suitable to their several capacities and condition."* At first this school was maintained by annual subscriptions, but in 1720 John Everett, William, Lord Digby, Digby Cotes, clerk, vicar of Coleshill and John Brooks, innholder, became trustees of a charity *"theretofore given by Simon, Lord Digby for the support and maintenance of the charity school already established in Coleshill, for the educating of poor girls in the Christian religion, as it is professed in the Church of England, and in reading, writing, arithmetic, and in works proper for women."*

In 1672 William Harvey had *"set up and built upon a part of waste of the manor of Coleshill a convenient house for the relief and habitation of two poor widows to inhabit."* This charity was still in existence in 1823.

Mention is also made of *"a messuage, cottage or tenement divided into three tenements called by the name of the Almshouse,*

141

with the garden and orchard thereto belonging and adjoining at the lower end of the Town of Coleshill."

At the time when the report was compiled, *"the old buildings being ruinous were lately taken down and upon the site have been erected one large house and two small ones. The large house contains three sleeping-rooms and two lower rooms appropriated to the use of poor travellers, and three other rooms occupied by a man and his wife, who are put to take care of the travellers, and have the benefit of a large garden belonging to the house."* This was part of the Grammar School Trust.

The interest from £500 given by William Lord Digby in 1694 continued to be spent, as he had directed, *"first and principally in laying out yearly or as often as need be required, the sum of £2 10s to buy bibles, common prayer books, the book called Whole Duty of Man, and such like books of practical divinity as should be thought convenient to be distributed. among such poor inhabitants of Coleshill as could read ."* £5 was to be spent *"in physic and things necessary to recover health for such poor persons of the said parish as by reason of their poverty should be exempt from payment to the church and the poor."*

Trustees were also permitted to *"employ yearly £5 for clothes for such widows or other poor housekeepers within the parish as should be in want and had been industrious and painful when able to work and had constantly frequented the church, and had been of sober and peaceful demeanour among their neighbours and not given to pilfering, scolding, drunkenness and other misdemeanour ...and upon further trust to employ £4 in teaching and instructing young girls, daughters of such poor people aforesaid, to spin, knit, sew, and do other just and lawful acts and things whereby they would in some measure be rendered cable of getting an honest livelihood. Also teaching the sons of such poor people to write and cast accounts, so far as to render them capable of being bailiffs or servants to some gentlemen, or to be put out to some honest trade."*

In addition £6 should be used for the *"setting out yearly of one boy, the son of some poor person inhabiting within the said parish, principally such boy as should be fatherless or motherless, or both, who could say the whole Church catechism without book, and read intelligibly, and write and cast accounts as aforesaid, and had behaved himself well."* At the trustees' discretion, any surplus could be spent *"on furnishing some apprentice in the parish, or on setting him up in trade, or buying him work tools."*

Another charity, established by Mrs. Offalia Rawlins in 1694, also continued to benefit the instruction of *"the younger girls and sons of poor people, as well as the apprenticing of a boy "in the second of each successive three years."* In each third year £3 was to be spent on clothes for poor widows, and the remainder of the money on *"physics and other necessary things."*

A charitable bequest, Adamson's Charity, was set up in May 1730. A baker was paid 15s. annually for bread, *"supplied by him on the first Sunday in every month, in small loaves, which are distributed at the church, by the churchwardens amongst the most needy of the parish."* A similar bequest, Orton's charity, mentioned in the same deed, was established for the laying out of bread on St. John's day. The commissioners commented that the distribution had for many years been neglected, and ought to be resumed.

Several charitable trusts, set up during the Georgian period did not specify the exact purpose but left the trustees to decide how best to spend the money for the benefit of deserving poor parishioners.

Gradually, in the 19th and 20th centuries, the various charities were gathered into the Simon, Lord Digby (Relief in Need) Charity. The last to be absorbed was the delightfully named Coleshill Lying in Charity, also known as the Lying in Club and in its rules referred to as the Society.

According to Charity Commission records, this Society was founded in 1789 and in 1832 the minute book and rules and regulations were rewritten *"as recollected by several members",* because the original minute book had been lost. The undated printed rules of the Society state that it was intended for the benefit of *"virtuous, sober and industrious wives and mothers".* One rule states that *"no person of bad character or residing more than five miles from Coleshill is eligible as member of this society."*

As well as medical care, every member received four shillings as soon as she began her lying-in, plus the loan of a testament and a bundle of linen provided by the Society. The linen had to be returned clean to the Steward after one month, together with the testament and a shilling was given on the return of these items.

143

Rule 5 shows that the subscription to members who wished to benefit from the Society is the same in the rewritten minute book and in the printed rules: two shillings and sixpence for enrolment and then six pence to be paid on the first Wednesday in every month.

Rule 6 is significant: *"Each member of the Society is required to take her infant (to the surgeon who attends her) to be vaccinated when not under three, nor over six months old. The neglect of this rule subjects her to be expelled from the Society altogether."*

Dr. John Barker, one of the Society's Medical Officers had published a book in 1769: 'The nature of inoculation explained, and its merits stated' and it was his conviction of the efficacy of inoculation, that gave rise to rule 6. Inoculation involved spreading matter from a smallpox scab onto an open cut in the skin, the most effective preventive measure before Edward Jenner discovered vaccination in 1796. This involved inoculation using matter from cowpox scabs, 'vacca' being the Latin word for cow.

The fact that the word 'vaccination' is used in the printed rules proves that they were issued or revised after 1796, and that Dr. Barker had accepted Jenner's treatment, which was by no means the case with all medical men!

In 1972 the name of the Society still contained the words 'married women', but in 2001, when its assets were transferred to the Simon, Lord Digby (Relief in Need) Charity, it is called the Charity for Sick and Pregnant Women, demonstrating a less moralistic attitude towards women in need.

Money spent during the last few years of the original Society included help towards the purchase of a washing machine for a divorced mother of four children under seven years, one of them still in nappies and two being nocturnally enuretic. One of the last few items of expenditure involved a particularly sad need: £50 to help with the funeral costs of two small sons.

CHAPTER 14.

THE POOR OF COLESHILL

THE WORKHOUSE
"Theirs is yon House that holds the parish poor,
Whose walls of mud scarce bear the broken door;
There where the putrid vapours, flagging, play
And the dull wheel hums doleful through the day;
There children dwell who know no parents' care;
Parents who know no children's love dwell there!
Heart-broken matrons on their joyless bed,
Forsaken wives and mothers never wed;
Dejected widows with unheeded tears,
And crippled age with more than childhood fears;
The lame, the blind, and, far the happiest they!
The moping idiot and the madman gay."

Description of the workhouse from 'The Village' by George Crabbe, 1783.

For many years the care of the poor was considered the churches' moral duty although whether they performed it was a matter of luck as there were no laws to ensure that it was carried out. Problems such as vagrancy were dealt with particularly harshly.

After the Dissolution of the Monasteries between 1536-39, parishes were obliged to provide for the impotent poor and to collect a poor rate from the more prosperous parishioners. In 1572 the Overseers Act was passed and in 1598 Justices were appointed as overseers of the poor and empowered to set the able-bodied poor to work, to establish almshouses for the old and infirm and to apprentice paupers' children. In 1601 the Poor Law Consolidation Act was introduced and became the basis of all Poor Law administration for the next 200 years. As there was a huge demand for help from the poor, the parishes would only give support to those legally entitled to it. Some disabled paupers were allowed to beg within strict limits, provided they had first obtained a licence from the magistrates.

145

THE WORKHOUSE AND WORK

Coleshill's poorest parishioners would have been consigned to the workhouse, a long narrow building with others, including the male dormitory and the local lock-up behind it and a large garden beside it. This was just off the High Street in what was then called Workhouse Lane, now Blythe Road. Although considerable stigma attached to workhouse life, there was growing awareness among the middle classes, via accounts in novels like 'Oliver Twist and 'The Old Curiosity Shop' plus heartrending verses like 'Christmas Day in the Workhouse' of the often inhuman conditions. Coleshill workhouse seems to have been one of the better ones.

As the name suggests, able-bodied paupers in the workhouse were expected to work in return for food and shelter. Apart from this, they also baked bread, brewed ale, kept their own pigs and probably chickens. They ate a considerable amount of cheese and there was milk for the children The Accounts for 1757 show that a pig was bought for £1.8.0d and later accounts of 1788 show that the workhouse purchased seed for onions, leeks, carrots and melons and sold its surplus vegetables. The inmates also grew potatoes, an important crop since the cost of wheat rose dramatically during the French Wars, so they were used as a substitute for bread, as an extract from a draft letter to the Poor Law Commissioners makes clear:

"We further consider that with the benefit arising from the garden ground for making an abundance of vegetables and to spare, we are thereby enabled, comfortably, to lessen the consumption of bread."

Some paupers also worked outside the workhouse, including men who were living outside but receiving money from the Poor Rate. According to a letter to the Poor Law Commissioners, the men mainly worked on the roads:

"In respect to employment of our able bodied poor whenever any are out of work we have an ample supply of work for them on the highways belonging to our own parish, having about 26 miles of

146

highways and carriage or draft roads, but always giving them considerably less rate of wages that can be obtained by independent labours and thereby keep them employed until they can obtain for themselves more beneficial employment."

Women were sent to work in the fields at harvest time and their payment was put towards the workhouse running costs. Some are also recorded as receiving payment for nursing and although not specifically mentioned, this could well have included wet nursing as several inmates were the mothers of infant children. Children up to the age of 10 or 12 years of age were employed in picking stones which were later sold to the turnpikes for road mending, at 8d per load!

Between 1802 and 1804 a Spinning School was set up to provide work for pauper girls. It bought 20 spinning wheels to spin flax and woollen yarn and although the school was not financially successful, showing a regular deficit, the accounts recorded:

"that the reductions in the weekly payments and the children's instruction in the laudable industry are considered an ample recompense and compensation for the deficiency."

After the age of 10 or 12 the children were likely to be apprenticed often outside the parish

Payments were also made to the poor living outside the workhouse. Until the end of the 18th century accommodation for the poor was generally available but with the Enclosure Acts many farm labourers' cottages were taken from them and pulled down. The birth rate rose and soldiers returning from the Napoleonic wars led to

much overcrowding and unemployment. Coleshill also had to pay other parishes for the care of its poor. Among the examples recorded were:

Widow Mammet	Shustoke
Widow Finch	Bedworth
2 Bastard children Coates	Dordon
Boy Wakelins	Curdworth
Boy Barlins	Packington

SETTLEMENT AND REMOVAL

In 1662 the Act of Settlement and Removal ensured that anyone arriving in a parish without right of settlement would be removed within 40 days unless they rented a £10 tenement or had some other way of proving that they would not become a charge on the parish. The parish where you were born was your place of settlement, an important right as the certificate of settlement was comparable to a present day passport.

From 1685 any newcomer had to give the overseers written notice of arrival and from 1691 this would be recorded in the parish book. A later Act of 1691 allowed paupers to stay in any parish providing they had a settlement certificate from their own parish guaranteeing to take them back if they became chargeable.

The applications certainly did not mince words over the status of undesirables due to be resettled and there was little tolerance of anyone pursuing an alternative lifestyle. One from Sussex records: *"Rogue and vagabond Joseph Horton who had been found wandering abroad and sleeping in barns was ordered to be returned to Coleshill his legal place of settlement."*

A newcomer could also apply to the local magistrates for a right of Settlement and was often successful if he had a skilled trade or was an employed labourer with a wife and family. The young who gained apprenticeships in parishes away from their birthplace took their new workplace as their place of Settlement. One such apprentice applied to the magistrates to be resettled in Coleshill as, after serving two years of his apprenticeship as a pearl button maker, his master enlisted in the army and the business closed. His application reads: *"William Johnson having served two years out of seven of his apprenticeship when his master listed for a soldier is asking for settlement in Coleshill, his place of birth."*

Unsuccessful applicants were removed for fear that they would become a charge on the parish and pregnant women were dispatched particularly rapidly, since if they gave birth in the parish, their offspring had right of Settlement there. One entry records unemotionally that *"Mary Wheeler being pregnant is ordered to be removed to the parish of Hanbury her place of legal settlement."*

APPRENTICES

Apprenticeships were a convenient way of reducing the poor rate as these pauper children were usually apprenticed in other parishes. They were welcomed as a source of cheap labour in the rapidly expanding manufacturing industries in Birmingham and the Black Country. Apart from the legal fees, the parish paid the master an apprenticeship fee ranging from £1.00 to £5.50 for instructing the youngster in his trade and the apprentice received two sets of clothes, one for work and one for Sunday. The earliest records of apprenticeships for Coleshill paupers are dated 1694 when there were two. By 1729 there was only one but between 1741 and 1746 the number rose to three and then to eight from 1760 to1768. Many of the children at this time were apprenticed in the silk weaving and ribbon weaving trades around Coventry and the numbers continued to rise dramatically so that from 1769 to 1789 there were 27 apprentices and 42 for the following decade. 96 of those youngsters were apprenticed in Birmingham and the Black Country, the highest proportion in the gun trades, such as gun locksmiths, stock makers and barrel borers

In the early 19th century the numbers again rose sharply; between 1800 and 1810 there were 52 apprentices but from then on the numbers began to fall; to 26 from 1810-1820, down to 24 in the next decade and only 8 between 1830 and 1836.

The apprenticeships in the gun trades fell noticeably thanks to the ending of the Napoleonic wars and although the Black Country still welcomed the poor children of Coleshill, a growing number was drawn into local trades.

Hatters and felt makers went to Atherstone, ironmongers to Nuneaton, bricklayers and brick makers to Kingsbury, frame work knitters to Hinckley, cordwainers (or shoemakers) to Maxstoke, tailors and cotton makers to Coleshill and even a surgeon in Tamworth.

Some of the girls went to Joseph Peel's cotton mills in Fazeley and were apprenticed as cotton weavers or spinners. Others were apprenticed in the art of housewifery but overall, relatively few girls were apprenticed and the account books show that most were put into service by private agreement with the overseer and the churchwardens.

In all over 200 pauper children were apprenticed legally. With the population growing rapidly, rising illegitimacy, increasing industrialisation and a decline in Coleshill's coaching and market trade, apprenticeships were an ideal way of reducing the number of pauper children in the parish. It is doubtful if their parents ever saw the children again. Although apprentices were a source of cheap labour, many of these young adults were ill-treated and few would believe their word against their master's, a situation reflected in Dickens' emotive account of Oliver's apprenticeship in 'Oliver Twist'.

However, the indenture was a legal document, binding on both sides. Masters found guilty of cruelty would have the indenture cancelled

as would apprentices whom a magistrate had found to have ignored instruction or disobeyed orders.

INDENTURE

County of *Warwick* to wit.

WHEREAS complaint hath been made before us two of his Majesty's justices of the peace in and for the said *county* by *Eleanor Clarke* apprentice to *William Simpson Cotton Work of the Parish of Nuneaton* in the said *County Warwick* that he the said *William Simpson* hath misused and ill-treated ~~him~~ the said apprentice, and particularly *hath beat her the said Eleanor Clarke and hath kept her without necessary provisions*

And whereas the said *William Simpson* hath appeared before us in pursuance of our summons to that purpose, but hath not cleared himself of any from the said accusation and complaint, but on the contrary the said *Eleanor Clarke* hath made full proof of the truth thereof before us upon Oath; We therefore by these presents do discharge ~~him~~ the said *Eleanor Clarke* of and from ~~his~~ apprenticeship to the said *William Simpson* any thing in the indenture of apprenticeship made betwixt them, or otherwise howsoever, to the contrary notwithstanding. Given under our Hands and Seals the *Twelfth* Day of *February* in the Year of our Lord One Thousand Seven Hundred and *seventeen*,

Apprentice Eleanor Clarke's indenture is cancelled in February 1817 after her master starves and beats her.

Despite the safeguards, a harsh working environment and frugal living standards were widespread before the 1833 Factory Act designed to make the apprentices' conditions more humane.

151

NATIONAL EVENTS WHICH SWELLED THE NUMBERS OF POOR PEOPLE COLESHILL.

Several national events massively affected the economic conditions throughout Britain and led to growing hardship for people already close to the breadline. Coleshill, as a market town heavily dependent on agriculture and its related trades, would have suffered more than most from these events.

In 1793 the French wars led to massive increases in the price of food especially wheat which more than doubled by the end of the war. Enclosure meant that farmers could maximise output but they passed little of their profits to their labourers and to the markets. Many labourers also lost their cottages and their right to graze animals on common and waste land. New machinery was killing off many cottage industries such as spinning and weaving which had boosted labourers' incomes.

In 1815 at the end of the Napoleonic wars, demobilised troops flooded back onto the labour market, triggering mass unemployment. Poor harvests aggravated the slump while better transport and markets in Birmingham and the decline of local trade in areas like Coleshill also increased the poverty levels.

In 1816 the Game Law Act made poaching punishable by transportation denying many poor villagers a rabbit or pheasant to supplement their meagre diet. The population soared by 46%.

COLESHILL'S GROWING POVERTY LEVELS

The increase in poverty is evident from the rising sums which Coleshill parish spent on maintaining the poor throughout the Georgian era

The cost of maintaining the poor increased in the late 18th century:

1772	£ 450	1s 8d
1788	£ 712	3s 2d
1799	£1246	9s 3d
1803	£1660	16s 9d

WORKHOUSE ACCOUNTS

Looking through the accounts is a laborious task but well worth the effort. The entries range from the mundane: payments for bread and the everyday costs of supporting paupers and children living on the parish, to the unexpected; like fees for a knobstick (shotgun) marriage. Others were heart-breaking, for example the payment for three children's coffins and their burial. The overseers' accounts of the period include intriguing details of medical services, vaccinations, spectacles, tooth extraction and even the fee for attending an inquest.

Apart from the poor who lived in the workhouse, scores of other needy people required help; the old, infirm, widows both old and young, unmarried mothers, wives with ill or invalid husbands and those whose spouses had deserted them.

Like today's benefits claimants, most of the poor were well aware of their rights and the accounts show that there were many requests for help.

A SHOTGUN WEDDING
(KNOBSTICK WEDDING)

Susannah Taylor, a pauper, applied to the Magistrates for help as she was pregnant, naming George Laffield as her child's father. The constable was ordered to arrest him and they were subsequently married. The cost of this wedding, by special licence, appeared in the workhouse accounts and the marriage was also noted in the parish registers.

The examination of Sue Taylor	1s 0d
The warrant to apprehend the reputed father	1s 0d
Sp. at same time	6d
Sp. at Lovells when man was taken	1s 4d
The licence for the wedding	£1 13s 6d
The ring 4/-, the fees 7/6	11s 6d
Gave the married couple	£2 2s 0d

The following entry suggests that the high mortality rate among poor children was an accepted fact of life:

The price of coffins as approved at meeting 1 Oct 1825.

Infants to 5 years old	5s 6d
From 5-9 years old	8s 6d
From 9-14 years old	12s 0d
From 14 years old and upwards	14s 0d

Payments into the workhouse accounts came from many sources, much of the money from other parishes to pay for their poor who were living in Coleshill. The County Treasurer made payments for discharged prisoners who passed through the parish. Rents were paid on Lady Day and Michaelmas Day and when the overseers returned vagrants to their own parish the cost was reimbursed.

The Collector of Excise made payments for the wives of serving soldiers, with pensions paid to the workhouse overseers instead of the recipient, while money found when an inmate died was also taken. Various men made in-payments for bastard children and as no bastardy orders or orders for the arrest of these men were found, it is likely that they acknowledged paternity. From the amounts paid, it would seem that they were higher up the social scale than ordinary working men

Despite their matter-of-fact tone, many of the entries hint at a turbulent underclass, moving in and out of poverty and a range of heartbreaking human stories as riveting as any modern-day soap opera. What was the emotional background to the entry recording, "Husband's repayment of loan advanced to his wife when he ran away."? What sort of person was the apparently wilful and headstrong Sarah Hartill whose unpredictable life can be partly traced from her regular appearances in the magistrates' courts and workhouse records? This is what we know of her story.

SARAH HARTILL

Sarah's parents, James Hartill and Sarah Adderley, married in Nether Whitacre in 1773 and Sarah was baptised here in 1775. She was the second of their four children and first appears in the records in 1802 appearing before the Magistrates claiming that John Russell was the putative father of her expected baby, though no record

To the Constable of *the Parish of Coleshill in the said County* *or his lawful Deputy.*

WHEREAS, *Sarah Hartill* . . . . ⸺ ⸺ ⸺ ⸺ ⸺ ⸺ of *the Parish of Coleshill* in the faid County, fingle Woman, hath by her voluntary Examination, taken in Writing upon Oath, before me, *Heneage Earl of Aylesford* . . . ⸺ ⸺ One of his Majefty's Juftices of the Peace in and for the faid County, this prefent Day declared herfelf to be with Child, and that the faid Child or Children is or are likely to be born a Baftard or Baftards, and to be chargeable to the Parifh of *Coleshill* . . . ⸺ in the faid County, and that *John Ruffell now or late* ⸺ . . . of *the Parish of Over Whitacre* in the faid County *of Warwick* *Labourer* ⸺ ⸺ is the Father of the faid Child or Children : And whereas, *James Jolley on behalf* ⬛ of the Overfeers of the Poor of the Parifh of *Coleshill* ⸺ ⸺ ⸺ aforefaid, in order to indemnify the faid Parifh of *Coleshill* ⸺ ⸺ in the Premifes, hath applied to me to iffue out my Warrant for the apprehending of the faid *John Ruffell* ⸺ . . . ⸺ ⸺ I do therefore hereby command you, immediately to apprehend the faid *John Ruffell* ⸺ ⸺ ⸺ ⸺ and to bring him before me, or fome other of his Majefty's Juftices of the Peace, for the faid County, to find Security to indemnify the faid Parifh of *Coleshill* ⸺ ⸺ ⸺ or elfe to find fufficient Surety for his Appearance at the next General Quarter Seffions of the Peace, to be holden for the faid County, and to abide and per-form fuch Order or Orders as fhall be made, in Purfuance of an Act paffed in the Eighteenth Year of the Reign of her late Majefty *Queen Elizabeth*, concerning Baftards begotten and born out of lawful Matrimony.

Given under my Hand and Seal, the *14*[th] ⸺ ⸺ Day of *April* ⸺ ⸺ 180 *2*.

Aylesford.

Bastardy order of Sarah Hartill

appears of him being found. In 1803 she was awarded 1/6d per week for her child. Then in 1807 came another request for help in tracing a Thomas Copes, another putative father, but no record that he was ever traced. Three years later, after Sarah yet again appeared, pregnant, before the Magistrates, a bastardy order was issued for a Thomas Joiner to be brought before them but there is no record of him being apprehended either

In 1811 Sarah was living in the Workhouse with her 3 children. Samuel, Amelia and Phyllis. A year later Samuel was apprenticed as a gunlock filer to Moses Smith of Aston thus gaining settlement in that parish. Sarah and her two daughters remained in the workhouse

Names of persons in the Workhouse
at Lady day 1835 _ _ _ _ _   ages

Ashby Edward	54
Britton Thomas	57
Britton John	32
gone apprentice Cushion Thomas	11
Cushion William	8
Davis Maria	36
Davis William	6
Divett Abraham	80
Deebank Ann	7
runaway Horton Ellen	14 - aug 1835- p 101
Hartill Sarah	57 ran away July 9 - 35
Kittermaster George	63

The record of Sarah running away

until 1813 when only 3-year-old Amelia was left there. According to the parish rates, Sarah received the sum of 1/6d a week from 24th February 1813 until January 1819, living out. In 1821 she was still outside the workhouse but the overseers were paying 4 shillings a week to someone, presumably for employing her. Sarah seems to have had regular spells in the workhouse and is listed as being there in 1831, aged 57. In 1833 she is not listed but appears there again in 1834 with her age still recorded as 57,

This Indenture made the _Tenth_ Day of _October_

in the _Fifty second_ Year of the Reign of our Sovereign Lord _George the Third_ by the Grace of God, of the United Kingdom of Great Britain and Ireland, King, Defender of the Faith, and in the Year of our Lord 1812, WITNESSETH, that _Robert Harrison and Robert Robinson Overseers of the Church_ of the Parish _of Bakewell in the County of Derby_ AND _John Ferne and Edward Barker_

by and with the Consent of His Majesty's Justices of the Peace

Overseers of the Poor of the said _Parish_ whose names are hereunto subscribed, have put and placed, and by these Presents do put and place _Samuel_ for the said _Parish_ aged _ten_ or thereabouts, a poor Child of the said _Parish_ an _Apprentice to_ _Moses Smith of the parish of Bakewell in the County of Derby_

Farmer with him to dwell and serve, from the Day of the Date of these Presents, until the said Apprentice shall accomplish his full age of _twenty one years_ according to the Statute in that Case made and provided; During all which Term, the said Apprentice his said Master faithfully shall serve in all lawful Business, according to his Power, Wit, and ability; and honestly, orderly, and obediently in all things demean and behave himself towards his said Master and all his during the said Term. And the said _Moses Smith_ for himself, his Executors and Administrators, doth covenant and grant, to and with the said Church-Wardens and Overseers, and every of them, their, and every of their Executors and Administrators, and their, and every of their Successors for the Time being, by these Presents, that the he the said _Moses Smith_

the said Apprentice in the best Way and Manner that he can _in the Trade or Business of a Farm Servant_ shall and will instruct, or cause to be taught and instructed, _____

_____

_____

_____ And shall and will, during all the Term aforesaid, find, provide, and allow unto the said Apprentice, competent, and sufficient Meat, Drink, Apparel, Lodging, Washing, and other things necessary and fit for an Apprentice, during all his Executors and Administrators, to be done and performed, shall continue and be in Force for no longer Time than three Calendar Months next after the death of the said _Moses Smith_ in case the said _Moses Smith_ shall happen to die during the Continuance of such Apprenticeship, according to the provisions of an Act passed in the Thirty-second Year of the Reign of King George the Third, entitled, "An Act for the further Regulation of Parish Apprentices," And also shall and will so provide for the said Apprentice, that he be not any Way a Charge to the said _Parish_ or Parishioners of the same; but of and from all Charge shall and will save the said _Parish and Parishioners_ harmless and indemnified during the Term.

IN WITNESS WHEREOF, the Parties above said to these present Indentures, interchangeably have set their Hands and Seals, the Day and Year first above written,

Delivered in the presence of

157

The Indenture for Samuel Hartill

obviously due to an oversight. Beside her name is the note *'ran away July 9th 35'*, when she would have been around 60 and there is no record of her after this date.

Several others also ran away around this period, possibly because of the uncertainty during negotiations over the imminent closure of Coleshill workhouse before it was taken over by the Meriden Union.

THE CLOSURE OF COLESHILL WORKHOUSE

The workhouse closed in 1836 when the Board of Guardians of the Meriden Union took over part of it on a 14-year lease at £10 a year. The offices were to be used for the forthcoming Civil registration of Births, Marriages and Deaths which began in July 1837. The Meriden Union Workhouse took over responsibility for the care of Coleshill's paupers, probably an unpopular move because conditions in the Union workhouses were notoriously poor, particularly the food. The daily allowance for adults was 8 ounces of potatoes, 12 ounces of bread, 4 ounces of meat plus gruel, a sloppy mixture rather like porridge. Meat would be withdrawn as a punishment. Children under 9 had no official allowance.

One major cause of resentment was the segregation of families and children were only allowed to spend one hour a week with their mothers, on Sunday afternoons in the Mothers' Room.

Coleshill's workhouse seems to have been far less barbaric, so it was probably a sad day for the poor of the parish when it finally closed its doors.

Chapter 15

CONCLUSION

Visitors approaching Coleshill will have a fine view of a wonderful medieval church with a tall spire, that it is built on a steep hill above the river Cole Signposts indicate that it is an historic coaching town. The 'town plan' is simple, consisting of one long street stretching along the road between Lichfield and Coventry, crossed by another short street along the road between Birmingham and Nuneaton. The centre of the town displays fine Georgian houses and quite a collection of inns and public houses. Outside the newly restored market Hall is a unique set of stocks combining a pillory and whipping post, previously standing in front of a central market hall in Church Hill; this road linking the Coventry Road and Nuneaton Road. At the foot of Church Hill, on the corner, are the remains of the old 'Parish Pump'. Today Coleshill is at the nodal point of many major communication routes and the outskirts of the town are dominated by transport. However even a glance at the town indicates previous prosperity and because of the road system, many have concluded that the signs prosperity visible today were due to the Golden Coaching Age. The Georgian Group began a study designed to explore this hypothesis and to establish the actual reasons for the town's prosperity.

One of the earliest mentions of Coleshill was in an Anglo-Saxon document of 799AD when King Coenwulf held a council in 'Coleshelle'. The town appeared in the Domesday Book in 1086 where the demesne was in Royal hands. It then passed into several families until 1495 when it was granted to Simon Digby as a reward for a family loyal to the crown. Documentation proves that Coleshill was an important and flourishing market town through the middle Ages and according to visual evidence, it became still more prosperous in Georgian times. Whether or not this was due to the stage coaching, Coleshill was firmly placed on an historical map with fine houses and at one time 22 inns and hostelries.

Had George I travelled through his new kingdom in 1714, he would have had a most uncomfortable journey along hard, rutted roads in the summer and through heavy floods in the winter. The journeys would have been extremely slow. Towards the end of the century with the development of the new turnpike roads travelling would have been easier and more frequent, but certainly not available for many people because of the cost. Very few people travelled far from their own or nearest market town.

What did happen was that government agents were paid to survey the land; rich men and very occasionally women would travel and record their journeys in diaries. Certainly Coleshill has benefited from their experiences and records. Although Coleshill was on the Great North Road there is neither documentary evidence nor any timetables to suggest that it was really important as a major staging post. The Royal Mail certainly came through Coleshill twice a day and the stopping place was the fine Swan Inn at the turn of the century when the stagecoach was really the most important means of public travel. It is interesting to note however, that there are a lot of inns with wide coach entrances on the main High Street which could suggest coaching importance of some kind or that in some instances the entrance may have been constructed for the entrance of private carriages.

At the beginning of the Georgian Era George I would have seen large areas of common ground divided into strips where poor people farmed their own small piece of land. He would have seen the contrast between some magnificent houses and some unfit even for animals. If George IV had made the same journey 100 years later he would probably have travelled by steam train covering the distance much more quickly and at any time of the year. The common ground would mostly have gone and there would be small fields surrounded by hedges and ditches. The poor people living off the common ground would have gone to the large cities and towns or some may have worked for one of the farmers who owned the fields. This change throughout the whole country over a period of more than 100 years has a mirror image in Coleshill and its surrounding area.

Coleshill during this time had a workhouse for the deserving poor, although latterly it was seen as a disgrace rather than deserving to be part of the system. Coleshill people were cared for reasonably well by the 'parish' with apprenticeships and outwork being found for the able bodied, as well as an established vegetable plot for the inmates. All of this was to support the running costs. In cases of a woman with a child being taken into the workhouse, every endeavour was made to find a child's father in order to secure payment.

As the Georgian Era drew to a close more and more people were looking towards the workhouse for support. Unfortunately there is only documentary and photographic evidence available of the workhouse, as the buildings have been demolished. Any punishments imposed for misdemeanours have been scantily recorded but the stocks are a gruesome reminder of how the whole town could witness a punishment.

The visual impact of fine Georgian houses and inns in a small market town suggests wealth. The richest person in Coleshill was Lord Digby who was the lord of the manor. During the whole of the period the Digbys had been consolidating and reorganising their land in line with the revolutionary developments in agriculture. Field enclosure and new roads had altered the landscape enormously; this had brought increased wealth to the Digbys as well as to some other farmers in Coleshill and surrounding areas. New farms were built in the fields close to the town and more wealth was generated among Coleshill's middle classes of the town. The people who suffered from these changes were often the poor who were deprived of common rights and who were removed from the their homes and work. This often resulted in migration to the cities. This was undoubtedly true of Coleshill. At this time however, the population grew rather than decreasing. This was attributed to more food generally and an increased knowledge of disease prevention. Dr. Barker, an eminent physician of Coleshill, was at the forefront of inoculation and wrote papers describing his findings in 1769. Despite the apparent wealth of the town, it was now that the lord of the manor moved to his other estate at Sherborne Castle in Dorset.

Recently many of the known and listed Georgian buildings have been surveyed. This has revealed, almost without exception that the Georgian buildings that are so clearly visible are either built on much earlier foundations or have had a facelift in line with the fashions of the times. Towards the end of the century this could have been influenced by the presence of the then Vicar of Coleshill, brother of the lord of the manor. The greater affluence of the town population could also have been a factor, they also wanted to have a fashionable home and emulate the city societies.

This survey indicates that Coleshill was prosperous before the Georgian Era began and the research so far indicates that agriculture has paid a greater part than anything else to contribute towards this prosperity. In view of the evidence collected so far it appears that there are few links between Coleshill's Georgian prosperity and the golden age of stage coaching, even though these coincided. In the future further evidence may come to light to dispute or confirm this finding.

We are greatly indebted to the Local Heritage Initiative Grant which has made all our research possible, adding enormously to our increased knowledge of the small market town of Coleshill and the many secrets that have been unravelled. No doubt there are many more to be discovered in the future. In presenting this book we look forward to receiving at the Heritage Centre any comments and additional material in the coming years.

BIBLIOGRAPHY AND SOURCES

CHAPTER 1. Employment and Living Standards

Warwickshire County Records Office
Coleshill Library
Albion's People John Rule Longmans
The Georgians at Home Elizabeth Burton Longmans
From Ploughtail to Parliament Joseph Arch The Cresset Library
Century Hutchinson

CHAPTER 2. Roads, Turnpikes and Maps

The Antiquities of Warwickshire William Dugdale
Copied in 1765 from 1656 by John Jones
The Illustrated Journeys of Celia Fiennes c1682-1712 Edited Christopher
Morris
Warwickshire in 1790 Peter Lavery, Osprey (1974)
The Georgian Gentleman Michael Brander
Coleshill and the Digbys, 500 years of Manorial Lordship Colin Hayfield
and Andrew Watkins 1995
British Transport, An Economic Survey from the Seventeenth Century to
the Twentieth H.J.Dyos & D.H.Aldcroft Pelican Books
An History of Birmingham W. Hutton, F.A.S.S. Third Edition 1808 Loaned
by Margaret Manley
The Making of the English Landscape W.G.Hoskins
The Torrington Diaries 1781 - 1794 Vols. II and III Hon. John Byng Edited
by C. Bruyn Andrews
A Tour through the Whole Island of Great Britain 1724 - 1726 Daniel
Defoe
Birmingham Archaeological Society's Transaction. Vol. 64
Warwickshire Turnpike Trusts Arthur Cossons
Directory of Warwickshire 1828, Pigot and Co.
The Travellers' Guide through England and Wales Thomas Kitchen
Patterson's Roads 1771, 18th edition 1828 Edward Mogg
An Act for repairing the roads from Coleshill in the County of Warwick,
through the city of Litchfield, to Stone in the County of Stafford, and from
thence to the City of Chester 1729.

CHAPTER 3. Stage Coaching and the Royal Mail

The Mailcoach Men of the late 18th century Edmund Vale
Royal Mail F.George Kay
A Regional History of England; the West Midlands from AD 1000 Marie
B.Rowlands
Coaching Days in the Midlands Brian Houghton
The Coaching Age David Mountford
Coleshill Directory
A More Expeditious Conveyance Bevan Rider
The Coleshill Book by the Civic Society
Torrington Diaries, Volume 2
The World of Stamps and Stamp Collecting
In Turner's Footsteps David Hill

CHAPTER 4 Canals and Railways

Information on the Coleshill Agreement from the Internet at
www.canals.btinternet.co.uk.
Information on Curdworth including copy of old print from Geoff Arthurs
of Curdworth.

CHAPTER 5. Coleshill's Georgian Families:

The Baker Family.
Information from Civic Society Archives.
Photograph by permission of the vicar, Canon Richard Bollard.

The Digby Family.
Information and illustrations from 'Coleshill and the Digbys' (1995) by
Colin Hayfield and Andrew Watkins with permission.
Reproduction of painting of the Dean of Durham by Joshua Reynolds by
permission of The Lord Digby.

The Dugdale Family.
Information on the Dugdale family generously supplied by Sir William
Dugdale and Matilda May.
William Stratford Dugdale's Diaries, Merevale Hall, by kind permission of
Matthew Dugdale.

The Leeson Family.
Information from Jack Leeson.
Photograph from Civic Society Archives.

The Peach Family.
Prepared by Mary Leeson (née Peach) February 2003.
Drawing of Peach Cottage by her grandson Alex.

The Prosser Family.
Information from Richard Prosser.
Photographs from Civic Society Archives

The Fetherston Dilke Family.
Information from A Short History of Maxstoke Castle by permission of Michael Fetherston Dilke.

The Reading Family.
Information from Tony Reading and Madge Smith.

The Sumner Family.
Information and illustrations are taken from The Story of Typhoo (1990) by Kenneth Williams, by permission of Mr John Sumner.

The Tuckley Family.
Information from Joan Tuckley
Photograph from Civic Society Archives.

CHAPTER 6 Georgian Houses

Around Coleshill, the Archive Photographs Series, (Chalford, Stroud, Gloucestershire) J.Bland, and C.Hayfield, 1996.
Traditional Buildings of Britain: An Introduction to Vernacular Architecture, (Victor Gollancz Ltd., London). R.W.Brunskill, 1981,
Coleshill Remembered 2: The Victorian and Edwardian Town, (Spring Hill Publications, Arley, Warwickshire). B.Gascoigne and C.Hayfield. 1990.
Coleshill and the Digbys: 500 Years of Manorial Lordship, (Spring Hill Publications, Arley, Warwickshire) C.Hayfield and A.Watkins, 1995.
Coleshill Remembered 1: The Changing Townscape from the 1940's, (Spring Hill Publications, Arley, Warwickshire) E.Miller and C. Hayfield, 1989.

'On The Dating of English Houses from External Evidence', Field Studies, Vol. 2, No. 5, 537-577. J.T. Smith and E.M. Yates, 1968
Investigating Old Buildings, (Batsford, London). L.Smith, 1985.
The Architecture of England, (Batsford, London). D.Yarwood, 1963.

CHAPTER 7 Public Houses

Map of Georgian Inns by Sylvia Weatherstone, North Arden History, issue 15 2000.
Much material supplied by Peter Whipps and Lloyd Moon,
Civic Society Archives.
'Coleshill Remembered' Eric Miller and Colin Hayfield. 1989.

CHAPTER 8 Occupations.

Warwickshire Watermills. D.T.N. Booth
Windmills in Warwickshire. W.A. Seaby & A.C. Smith
Coleshill Parish Chest papers at W.C.R.O.
Coleshill Hall estate Accounts 1763-96, part of the Digby Archives at Sherbourne Castle supplied by A. Smith, Archivist
Census Rolls for 1811, 1821, 1831.
West's Directory 1830
Pigot's Trade directory 1828/29
Coleshill Chronicle 23/06/34

CHAPTER 9. Agriculture.

Beaties of England and Wales Vol. 15 1814 J. Britten F.S.A
General View of the Agriculture of the County of Warwick with observations on the means of its improvement Adam Murray 1813
General View of the Agriculture of the County of Warwick With observations on the means of its improvement Mr. John Wedge (of Packington) Jan 1794
Warwickshire in 1790 Peter Lavery 1974
Pigot and Co.'s Warwickshire Directory 1828/29
Commissioner's Minute Book for Coleshill Enclosure 1779 WCRO DRB100/132
Essay on Coleshill and Coleshill Heath Sept.18th 1711 Coleshill Archives - File 17.
We have drawn from previous research on the Digby family by Ann Batchelor.

CHAPTER 10. Churches

Details of St Leonard's Church, Nether Whitacre by kind permission of Tony Varnam, Hoar Farm, Over Whitacre

CHAPTER 12. Law, Order, Crime and Punishment

Crime and Society in England 1750-1900 Clive Emsley Heinemann
History of Warwickshire John Child
Warwickshire in 1790 Peter Lavery
A Picture of Warwickshire Life Peter Lavery
Warwickshire Douglas Hickman
The Local Historian's Encyclopedia John Richardson
The Short and Bloody History of Highwaymen John Farman
Coaching Days in the Midlands Brian Haughton
Warwick County Records
Birmingham County Records
Crime and Society in England 1750-1900 Clive Emsley

CHAPTER 13. Charities
Regulations of the Coleshill Lying-In Society: 1832 Warwick Records Office
Printed Regulations of the Society, undated: Coleshill Civic Society Archives
Dr John Barker: The Nature of Inoculation explained and its merits stated B.Law and J.Dale, 1769
Charity Commission Documents.

CHAPTER 14. The Poor of Coleshill
Warwick Record Office.

VALUE OF THE GEORGIAN £1 IN 2001

Year	Value
1714	£96
1730	£101
1750	£103
1761	£120
1781	£97
1801	£42
1820	£62
1841	£59

INDEX

Agrarian Revolution 103, 111
Angel 28-, 75
Apprentices 13, 52-, 84-,143-
Barker Family 4, 31, 46-, 144, 161, 167
Bibliography 163
Byng, John 6, 26-, 32, 163
Canals and Railways 41
Coach 29-
Coleshill Agreement 44, 164
Coleshill House 30, 67-
Court Leet 6, 133-
Curdworth 7, 23, 41-, 129, 139, 148, 164
Defoe, David 19, 21, 23, 163
Digby Family 12-, 30, 47, 57, 62, 67, 69, 76, 81-, 131, 141, 159-
Dilke Family 48, 165
Dugdale Family 20, 27, 50-, 165
Enclosures 105, 108
Fiennes, Celia 20, 163
George & Dragon 79-
Grammar School 6-, 46, 63, 114-, 141
Green Man 75
Grinning Contest 108-
Highwaymen 34, 37, 124, 128-, 167
Horse Racing 108
Leeson Family 51, 54, 75, 165
Leland, John 20, 100
Lying in Society 5, 141-
Mail Coaches 6, 33-, 129
Maps 18, 22-, 32, 72, 82, 84, 90, 94, 105, 116, 160
Market Hall 1, 48, 84, 93, 128-, 159
Mills 7, 55, 81-, 139, 150, 165
Money Values 168
Occupations 9, 11, 14, 54, 82, 86, 94, 111
Over Whitacre Church 116
Parish Church. 4, 36, 47-, 86, 112-, 141
Peach Family 52-, 165

Pillory 1, 6, 126, 128, 159
Population 9
Poverty 4-, 10, 14, 126, 142, 152, 154
Prosser Family 54-, 87, 165
Reading Family 55-, 165
Stocks 1, 4-, 124-, 159-
Stonebridge 6, 40, 65, 89, 97
Sumner Family 52, 57-, 165
Swan 4, 6, 26-, 63-, 76-, 88-, 104, 108-, 120, 160
Three Tuns 62, 64, 77-
Timeline 6
Tollhouse 22-
Torrington, Lord 26, 101, 163-
Tuckley Family 51, 59, 93, 165
Turnpikes 6, 17-, 65, 95, 105, 147, 160, 163
Wesleyan Chapel 4, 7, 114
Wheatsheaf 73
Workhouse 4, 7, 53, 74, 129, 131, 145-, 153-